THE
PROFIT
PLAY
BOOK

THE PROFIT PLAYBOOK
Stop Guessing. Start Growing.

Michael James Johnson

Published by Game Changer Publishing

Paperback ISBN: 978-1-968250-68-3
Hardcover ISBN: 978-1-968250-69-0
Digital ISBN: 978-1-968250-70-6

GAME CHANGER
PUBLISHING
www.GameChangerPublishing.com

To God —
Before anything else, I give You the glory.

You carried me when I was tired, steadied me when I was unsure,
and opened doors I never could have opened on my own. This book
is a reflection of Your grace, not my strength.

Thank You for trusting me with this assignment.

To my wife —
Your steady belief, love, and sacrifice made this possible.
You stood beside me through the long nights, the setbacks,
and the silent battles.
You are the heart behind everything I build.

To my three boys —
You are my why.
Every late hour, every hard decision, every ounce of grit
—I did it with you in mind.
May you always chase purpose over comfort,
and character over applause.

To my mom and dad —
Thank you for showing me what hard work, character, and
consistency really look like. Your example gave me the foundation
to build everything that's in these pages. I carry your lessons
with me every day.

And to my brother and every friend, mentor, and teammate who's
helped shape my journey—

Thank you. This book is part of your legacy, too.

Read This First

Just to say thanks for buying and reading my book, I've created some resources just for readers to help you start building profit faster and easier.

Scan the QR Code Here:

THE
PROFIT
PLAY
BOOK

Stop Guessing. Start Growing.

MICHAEL JAMES JOHNSON

Table of Contents

Introduction

I remember standing in my truck—invoice in one hand, phone in the other—wondering how I could be this busy and still not profitable. I had the calls. I had the team. But something was broken. I was stuck.

I didn't come from money. I didn't have a rich uncle or a business mentor showing me the way. What I had was grit—and a whole lot of lessons learned the hard way.

I've lived through the sleepless nights, the silent stress, and the moments when I'd close the door to my office just to cry—because I felt completely alone and didn't know who to talk to or what to do next.

If you're reading this and thinking, *I'm working nonstop, but there's still no money*, or maybe, *I'm making something—but I can't figure out how to grow it*, this book is for you. In it, I'm going to teach you the exact strategies I used to turn my HVAC business from a job that consumed me into a machine that runs without me.

This isn't a theory. These are real principles—learned from two decades in the trenches and from some of the most expensive business coaching you can imagine. I've simplified them and tested them across dozens of companies.

I wrote this because I know what it's like to be in the dark. I want to give you the light I wish I had when I started.

You're going to learn what actually moves the needle—the things that generate fast growth, consistent revenue, and freedom from being the babysitter of your business.

It all starts here: by shifting from being the operator to becoming the true owner of your business.

Let's get started.

How This Book Is Structured

Before we dive in, I want to give you a quick roadmap of what to expect.

In Chapter 1, "From Owner to Operator," we'll explore the mindset shift required to build a business that runs without you. This is where we dig into what it means to stop being the technician and start thinking like a true business owner. In Chapter 2, "Start With What Moves the Needle," I'll walk you through the fastest ways to create momentum in your business—strategies you can implement immediately to generate cash flow and stability. In Chapter 3, "Pricing for Profit," we'll talk about one of the most powerful levers in business: charging what you're actually worth. I'll break down real-world examples and how to overcome pricing fears that are keeping you broke.

In the following chapters, we'll cover service agreements, branding, sales, team-building, and exit strategies—each one designed to help you build a business that's both profitable and sustainable. Whether you're just getting started or scaling toward the multiple seven-figure mark, this structure is meant to help you take the right steps at the right time, with clarity and confidence.

Let's get to it.

CHAPTER 1

From Owner to Operator: Designing a Business That Doesn't Break Without You

As my business grew, I started noticing something unsettling: I wasn't as on top of things as I thought I'd be. In the beginning, I imagined that once I gained momentum, everything would naturally fall into place. I thought I'd have control over every moving part. That success would mean fewer headaches, not more. But reality had other plans.

I had all the information in my head—appointments, customer requests, open invoices, service follow-ups—but the problem? That's exactly where it stayed. As the business got busier, I started forgetting more tasks than I was remembering. I had plenty of potential and an incredible amount of customer support, but I was unintentionally creating chaos.

Then came the wake-up call that changed everything. A few years in, a customer mailed me a letter. (Yes, an *actual* letter—so I might be dating myself here.) But that letter turned out to be the greatest gift anyone had ever given me in business.

The customer wrote that while he believed I was honest and hardworking, he also noticed I was disorganized and unreliable. He pointed out that I was constantly canceling appointments—not because I was lazy or didn't care, but because I was overwhelmed. I was either swamped or I flat-out forgot. He told me that while he wanted to keep using my company, he simply couldn't trust that I'd show up when I said I would.

That letter stung. Bad.

I sat with it for a while, feeling the weight of what he was saying. He wasn't attacking me—he was telling me the truth. My business wasn't everything I had dreamed it would be, and it was my own lack of organization holding me back. But as painful as it was to read, that letter became fuel. It pushed me to make my company into what I had always envisioned.

I realized that if I didn't fix this, my business would never grow beyond a certain point. I needed to figure out where the holes were, because a business is like a bucket—if there are leaks, your customers will slip right through.

From that moment on, I made it my mission to plug every hole I could find. Whether it was through a proven system, a dedicated employee, or the right software, I had to create structure. No more relying on memory or last-minute scrambling.

That letter was a harsh lesson, but it taught me something every business owner needs to understand: painful growth and negative feedback should never deter you. If you let it, it can be the catalyst that takes you from struggling to thriving.

My First "Big" Business Opportunity

That lesson prepared me for another defining moment in my journey—the first big business opportunity that put my skills (and my systems) to the test.

I was barely out of my 20s, just getting started in the HVAC industry, when I landed my first real service contract. A family called about an AC unit that wasn't cooling properly. I showed up with enthusiasm and optimism—but very little understanding of how to run a business.

At first, it seemed like a straightforward service call, but I quickly realized that being a great technician wasn't enough. This wasn't just about fixing the AC—it was about managing expectations, providing clear communication, and making sure I was tracking everything on the business side.

The problem? I didn't have systems in place. I had no formal way to track inventory, service calls, or customer follow-ups. I was still working off a notepad and my memory, and as the day went on, I could feel the weight of my disorganization catching up with me.

I spent hours on that job, making sure the customer was happy, but in the back of my mind, I knew I was falling behind on everything else. There were other appointments I needed to confirm, invoices I hadn't sent, and parts I was running low on—but I had no structure in place to keep up with it all.

In the end, the customer was satisfied with the fix, but I was exhausted—not just physically, but mentally. The emotional toll of trying to juggle everything without the right processes was overwhelming.

That day, I realized something that would shape the rest of my business journey: It's okay not to have all the business answers at first. But if you don't put the right systems in place, you'll burn yourself out.

Success isn't just about being good at your trade—it's about building a business that can handle the work efficiently.

From that point forward, I was determined to stop operating on memory and instinct alone. I started implementing processes to ensure no customer was forgotten, no appointment was missed, and no job fell through the cracks. I invested in software to track service calls, set up reminders for follow-ups, and eventually hired a team to help manage operations.

That's when I truly started to scale.

It was one of the hardest lessons to learn, but also one of the most valuable insights I now share with other business owners:

> *You can be the best technician in the world, but if you don't put the right systems in place, you'll always struggle to grow.*

If I had to start all over again today, I know for a fact I could build a successful HVAC company even faster than before. Not because I'd work harder, but because I'd work smarter.

In business, we like to think of success as simply working hard and providing great service. But the truth is, a great technician without great systems will always struggle.

For me, reality hit hard when I realized my business wasn't just leaking customers—it was hemorrhaging them. A business is like a bucket that holds water, and if that bucket has holes, your customers will leak out. Well, my bucket didn't just have a few leaks—it was worse than Swiss cheese.

I had a lot going for me. I was honest, hardworking, and people liked me. But that didn't matter when customers couldn't get a hold of me, when I showed up late—or worse, when I forgot appointments altogether. The more I tried to do everything myself, the worse it got. I thought I was running the business, but in reality, the business was running me. And not in a good way.

I had quite a few holes in my operation:

The Scheduling Nightmare

I had no proper scheduling system. I relied on memory, scattered notes, and my phone's calendar, which meant I was constantly double-booking myself, showing up late, or canceling appointments altogether. Some days, I had service calls booked across town from each other, wasting hours in drive time. Other days, I had three appointments stacked too close together, leaving no time to breathe, let alone grab lunch.

I needed my schedule to manage me—not the other way around. That meant mapping out calls efficiently, so I wasn't zigzagging across town. It meant creating structured time slots instead of cramming jobs in wherever they'd fit.

The Phone Call Chaos

I also needed someone to answer the phone. At first, I thought answering it myself was the best way to stay in control. But it was a disaster.

If I rushed through calls to get to the next job, I wasn't getting enough details from the customer. That meant showing up unprepared, which wasted even more time on site.

On the flip side, if I stayed on the phone too long trying to troubleshoot, I wasn't booking enough appointments to keep my business profitable. I was essentially giving away free consulting while losing the chance to close actual service calls.

I needed a dedicated person to handle the phones—someone who could book jobs efficiently while making sure I had all the details I needed. I also needed proper scheduling software—not a whiteboard in my garage, not a stack of sticky notes, but a real system that could track everything in one place.

The Stocking System Disaster

Then there was inventory. I can't even count how many times I showed up to a job thinking I had the part I needed—only to find out I didn't. That meant either making an extra trip to the supply house or rescheduling the appointment altogether. And every time that happened, it cost me money.

I needed a stocking system that actually worked—one where I could track what parts I had, what I was running low on, and what needed to be reordered before I found myself empty-handed in front of a frustrated customer.

Once I saw all the holes in my business, I realized I had two choices:

1. Keep winging it and hope things magically get better.
2. Get serious about building real systems.

I chose the second option.

I started by putting structure in place—scheduling software that mapped out my calls properly, a call handler who could book appointments efficiently, and a tracking system for my parts and inventory. I created processes so my business no longer relied solely on my memory or last-minute scrambling.

The difference was like night and day.

- I was no longer running around town wasting time between service calls.
- My customers weren't waiting forever to get a callback.
- I wasn't overbooking or missing appointments.
- I stopped losing money on repeat trips for parts I should have had.

For the first time, I felt like I was in control of my business instead of drowning in it.

And the best part? Once I had these systems in place, growth finally became possible. Instead of running around like a one-man circus, I could focus on scaling the business the right way.

If you're reading this and feel like you're barely keeping your head above water—like you're doing all the work but still spinning your wheels—it's time to look at your bucket.

- Where are your leaks?
- Are you booking jobs inefficiently?
- Are customers falling through the cracks?
- Are you spending more time fixing your own disorganization than actually growing your business?

Success isn't just about working hard. It's about building a system that allows your business to run efficiently, so you can scale without losing your sanity.

Once I figured that out, everything changed.

The first thing to understand when you're talking about designing a business—not just creating a job—is making the mindset shift that you're a business owner, not a technician. Typically, when someone starts a business, they unknowingly begin as a technician.

What I mean by that is, they might say something like, "I can fix an air conditioner, so maybe I should open an HVAC company." But when you do that, you're starting off as the technician—the person doing the actual work. That's not the ideal way to start a business. The ideal approach is to think, *I know how to make a cake, maybe I should open a bakery.* Then you write down your recipes, open the bakery, and hire someone to bake the cakes while you oversee and run the business.

That's the proper way to do it. It's a real mindset shift. That was one of the biggest lessons for me when I first started my business. I didn't understand that I was just being the technician—I knew how to fix air conditioners.

I thought, *Hey, I've got a business in a box. I can fix air conditioners, and I can go out on my own.* But that couldn't be further from the truth. When you start a business, you have to become a business owner, especially if your goal is to create something more than just another job. Most of the time, people start businesses to blaze their own trail, to gain more freedom, or to escape the nine-to-five grind. But if you don't structure it as a business, you end up just trading one job for another—only this time, you're working even more hours. That's the trap a lot of business owners fall into.

You have to adopt that business owner mindset from the very beginning. Part of that shift involves recognizing that you'll need to get someone else to do the work with you, or for you. There's often a lot of what I call "head trash" or limiting beliefs that come into play when a business is started. Those need to be eliminated right at the beginning. We'll get into that a bit more later.

But for now, just understand this: your highest value as a business owner lies in being a supervisor, a leader, and a visionary—not in doing the technical work. You're the one with the dream, the vision, the drive to change the world. You want to blaze your own trail. You carry the risk, the passion—that makes you the ideal leader for your business. But you can't lead your business if you're stuck in the trenches, doing everything yourself, wearing all the hats. That's one of the main reasons—if not the reason—why most business owners get bogged down in the day-to-day grind. They start the business expecting to do it all.

If your mindset is, "I know how to do this, so I'm going to start a business doing this," then you'll be doing it every day, all day. And because you'll also have to handle everything else that comes with running a business, you'll end up working far more hours than you would have in a regular job. So it's a total shift—from "I'm going to start a business and do the job," to "I'm going to start a business, train others to do the work, and take on a supervisory role."

And then, maybe eventually, you sell the business or transfer it to your children. It all depends on what your reason is. But everything, of course, starts with a mental shift.

I gave an example earlier about a baker who says, "Hey, I know how to cook, I know how to make cakes, so I'm going to open a bakery." And then that baker gets stuck baking. The problem with that is you're never going to be free.

I just heard from a friend of mine—I was doing some consulting—and he told me he had a record month in his business. He made more money this month than he's ever made. But as he kept talking, he shared that he's working seven days a week, twelve hours a day.

When I asked him, "Is this what you wanted when you started the business?" he said, "Of course not, but I love the money."

I said, "Okay, but how does your wife feel? How do your children feel?"

He replied, "Oh, they hate it."

It's even causing tension in his marriage. And that's not the point. Sometimes, when we forget our "why"—or put ourselves in the wrong role—we end up getting something out of the business that we never really wanted. It's not always about the money.

We have to return to our "why." Rarely does anyone start a business thinking, *I want to work all the time.* If you think back to everyone you know who has started a business—or even to yourself—you didn't sit down and write, *"This is what I want: to have no free time to spend with my family."*

No one wants that. But if you don't set yourself up from the beginning to be in the right leadership role, then every time you create a new product or offer a new service, you're just adding more work to your plate. The more the business grows, the more customers you have— and the more customers you have to deal with.

So every day actually adds more to your workload. This is why the ideal startup method is to document your process. Returning again to the example of the baker, the ideal startup mindset would be to document the recipe, train bakers on how to do everything, and then manage the business. It's not about disappearing from the business— it's about placing yourself in the proper role. You start that by writing down every single step you do each day.

Eventually, you'll have a document you can hand to someone and say, "This is how it's done." Then, you observe the process. As mistakes happen or issues arise, you improve the system.

That's the right mindset. And you don't have to have had that mindset from the start. If you're reading this and saying, "Well, I started my business five years ago, and this is 100% me," it's not too late. The real change happens the moment you shift your mindset from operator to owner.

So what are the costs of stepping into that leadership role? Sometimes we say, "Okay, I'm going to be the boss. I'm going to be the visionary. I'm going to be the leader. And I'm going to let others do the technical work or handle the day-to-day." But that often comes with mixed emotions. I'll be the first to admit: when I stepped aside, after running my business for ten years, I had made the mindset shift, but I still didn't fully let go.

So all I did was become a micromanager. And one of the costs of micromanaging is that no one in your company ever learns to make decisions. So you just end up creating more problems for yourself. The team becomes dependent on you, and they're afraid to act. The business bottlenecks around you—even when you're not there, it's almost like you are there—because they're scared of making a mistake. So, the mindset shift starts with understanding: *Hey, I'm going to be an owner, not an operator*. But it doesn't end there.

It's about letting go—truly letting go—and allowing others to try and fail. And it's a process. Having been in the trades for over twenty years, I know how difficult it is to train people. We are often running a mile a minute and don't have time to slow down. Instead of taking the time to train people, we do things ourselves and put training off. All this does is keep you trapped longer.

The mindset shift is only the beginning. So, what is the definition of a self-sustaining business? What does it mean to start a business that sustains itself? I had a business coach who told me something one day that changed my life forever.

He said, "Michael, if you got sick today and were sick for six months—if you were in the hospital and couldn't answer your phone—what would happen to your business?"

"It would end," I told him. "It would completely stop."

And he said, "Well, you don't have a business. You have a job."

That changed my mindset forever, because I thought I was running a business. I had employees. But they were so dependent on me, so paralyzed, that, truly, if I wasn't there, it wouldn't run. And that's the definition of a job.

There's nothing wrong with a nine-to-five. But if you are investing your entire life savings and all your time into a business, then turn it into one. If you're going to have a nine-to-five job, have a nine-to-five job—without the risk, the financial burden, and the stress.

What are the first areas to delegate when you say, "Okay, I'm an owner. I want to be an owner. I don't want to be a technician"? Where do you even start? Often, the best place is to delegate someone to answer the phones. Missed calls mean missed revenue. Get someone answering that phone first.

If you're a technician—a plumber under someone's sink fixing pipes—you can't answer the phone properly. Did you know that trust is immediately built when the phone is answered quickly? How much trust do you lose when your phone goes to voicemail? Get someone to answer that phone. Take that stress off yourself. And of course, phone calls should be answered immediately—not as a background task.

One of the first things you need to do is to map out every single step of the customer journey, from first contact to follow-up. Everyone reading this book has probably been to a restaurant. How many steps are there in a restaurant experience? When you walk in, what happens? What if the food is delicious, but when you walked in, no one greeted you, or it took 30 minutes to find a seat—or an hour to bring the dessert?

This is the number one issue in small home service businesses. The technical knowledge and skill are there, but growth is limited because the business lacks proper systems. So, what are the steps in your business? From the very beginning—from the moment they call to the time the job is complete—someone has to fill the role at every step along the way. And that's when you begin to make your hiring decisions.

Okay, so what are some of the red flags? If you're saying, "Okay, I hear you, Michael. I'm really into this. I really want to do this. I want to change my mindset," what are some of the red flags in our own minds? Because, a lot of times, we don't recognize our own pitfalls. Here's one of them:

A red flag is: "I'd like to delegate that, but this particular thing—I have to do it because it's really delicate." That's a red flag. That's a trapped mindset.

I hear this all the time from clients, but you don't have to do everything. If you're able to do it, someone else is able to do it. Even if someone does it a little slower or with less capability, it still frees you up when you hire it out.

Even if someone else can do it a little slower or not quite as well as you—that's okay. Because it frees you up, and they can learn and get better. You didn't learn overnight. Don't expect someone else to, either. Let it go. That fear that no one can match your performance is a total lie we tell ourselves.

Typically, what I like to do when I'm consulting a business at the very beginning—and I'm trying to find out what needs to be fixed immediately—is ask a lot of really deep-diving, introspective questions. I ask over sixty questions in the first meeting when I'm consulting people, because, a lot of times, our deep-seated fears, our anxieties, the things holding us and our businesses back are hiding behind the first or second question. So, you have to take some time to really be introspective. Sit back and ask yourself: *What is working, and what's not?* Really dig deep. Write those answers down.

Write your fears down. Write your concerns down. Then find a way to fix them—no matter how scary it is. Because your business problems always stem from your own mindset. This is why some businesses grow very fast, and others struggle forever.

Identify your mindset blocks, your inefficient habits, and any area where you over-control things. This doesn't mean you disappear. I made a tremendous mistake when my business grew to a point where I was able to step back for the first time in my life. I had no idea what that meant. I was so free—I had been waiting for it for so long—that I actually disappeared from the business. That caused me to go back out into the field, and I pretty much lost almost all of my employees. So, it's not about disappearing and saying, "Hey, let them do it without checking," but about trusting them. Let it go—but verify that things are being done. Manage them. Just don't micromanage. Empower your people. Just don't abandon your people. Hopefully, that helps ease some of your fears.

Becoming a better leader and stepping into that role—changing your mindset—looks different for different people. The best thing you can do is start with your personal history. You're going to lead the way you were led. Unfortunately, a lot of times, we are products of our environment.

Let me give you an example. When I started my business, I had a van that someone gave to me. It was the worst, ugliest van a human had ever seen, but it was all I had. It was all I could afford. It would break down at least once a week. I remember the feeling of being completely defeated—broken down. And people didn't take the time. They just drove by. They would drive right past me on the road. They wouldn't even stop to help.

So, I decided I was going to help anyone I could. If I ever saw someone broken down on the road, I would stop and help, which is exactly what I did for many years.

Fast-forward to when my kids were growing up. One day, my ten-year-old was in the car with me, and we saw someone broken down on the side of the road. I said, "Hey, wait right here. I'm going to help." I ended up pushing the car off the road—actually, I pushed it into a ravine.

The two individuals who were in the car jumped out, and the car rolled into the ravine—into a lake. It wasn't my fault. It had nothing to do with me. There was something wrong with the vehicle. But my little boy looked at me when I got back in the car and said, "I will never push a car out of the road again."

So, what happened right there? My little boy made a life decision based on something he saw.

That could possibly become a roadblock for him in the future. And the reason I say that is because it happens to us, too. The things that block us when we're running a business—we have to dig into those, figure out what they are, undo them, and shift our mindset.

Sometimes, we have to dig into our own personal history. How were you led? By your mom? Your dad? Your old bosses? See, most great leaders are built. You're not necessarily born that way. If you're saying, "Hey, I didn't have a rich uncle who owned a business to teach me," or "I didn't have a professor to walk me through this," guess what? None of us did. And you're not going to be perfect at the beginning. That's why I'm writing this book—to teach you everything I've learned over the last twenty years. Because I definitely didn't have it all figured out in the beginning. We're all growing, and we're all learning.

So, returning to the struggle to let go, delegation is difficult. It's incredibly difficult because—if you're a founder of your business—your identity is tied to perfection. You have a dream of what this business is going to be. You see the business 100 years from now. You see the end result.

And when things in that business don't look like the end result—for example, during the first year or second year, when there are struggles—we panic and think the sky is falling down. That's why we don't like to delegate. But the truth is, a lot of times, things are ugly at the beginning. Sometimes, they're ugly in the middle. But you have to allow those failures. You have to allow those things to happen to get to where you want to be.

A lot of that is going to come from delegating and letting go. We have to learn how to trust our systems—not just our people. That's why I say, and in this book, I'm going to teach you how to create systems. How to create something that allows people to be as great as you would be if you were in that position.

We're not going to keep ourselves in that position. We're not going to micromanage and force people to be us. But we are going to learn how to create systems to help people become as great as they can be. And that's my story.

When did I start my business? I'm usually embarrassed to say this— I've been in business for twenty years at the time of this writing. But the first ten years were very, very difficult. I was doing everything. I was writing the invoices. I was answering the phone. I was calling people back. Doing social media ads. Handling customer service. I would often get burned out.

Every six months, I would burn out and disappear for a month and a half, because I was doing everything. I remember one day, I was hanging out with my brother on a Saturday, and I said, "Man, William, I don't even have time to tie my shoes." And that was the reality.

I was just so burnt out. It was ridiculous—and it didn't change until I changed my own mindset. In this book are all the things I learned to get out of that crazy situation and into a business that runs by itself, without me.

So, the biggest realization is this: you're not just a plumber—you're a plumbing business owner. You're not just an HVAC technician—you own an HVAC company. And ownership comes with different responsibilities than just doing the work itself.

One of the big mistakes I made was this: I remember, after ten years of being in business and working incredibly hard—delegating, getting past all my mental setbacks that had stopped me from delegating, all my micromanaging, all my fears—I finally did it. My business was running without me. And I didn't even know what to do, because I had never been in that position before.

It was something I had waited all my life to achieve, but I didn't know what running a business really meant. I knew what *doing* business meant. I knew how to fix air conditioners. I knew how to talk to customers. But now that I wasn't doing those things, I didn't know what to do. I was told to delegate, so what I did was just sit at home and watch *Star Trek* all day for weeks at a time. The money was coming in, the business was operating well, and unfortunately, I gave up too much control.

I just kind of let everything happen. I wasn't checking anything. And I actually worked my way back into what was basically a nine-to-five job. I lost all of my employees, except one.

I got back out into the field, and that's when I told myself: *You know what? The next time I get into this position—where I'm out of the day-to-day tasks and the business runs without me—I'm going to learn how to be a true owner. I'm going to know what to check, when to check it, and what to verify, so that I can be a good owner, not an owner who abandons the business and lets it fall apart.*

Now that we've uncovered the mindset needed to build a sustainable, profitable business, it's time to roll up our sleeves and make some real changes.

You don't need a five-year plan or a fancy degree—you need clarity, momentum, and the right plays to start winning now. In the next chapter, we're going to focus on what actually moves the needle in your business. These are the fast wins—the strategic shifts that generate real profit, quickly. Let's stop spinning our wheels and start stacking revenue.

CHAPTER 2

Start With What Moves the Needle

Forget fancy—double down on what works now.

When you step into the world of business, especially in the trades, you'll notice something pretty quickly: there's a pissing contest happening at every turn.

Business coaches, social media influencers, and even some of your competitors will shout from the rooftops about their seven-figure revenue. They'll tell you that if you're not hitting a million in revenue, you're doing something wrong.

And if you do hit seven figures? Guess what? The contest doesn't stop.

Now it's, "Well, are you at two million?"

Then, "You should be at five million by now."

And before you know it, you're chasing revenue like a dog chasing its tail—running faster, working harder, and stressing more—all while wondering why you're still not financially free.

Because here's the ugly truth nobody brags about in those revenue flexes: Revenue means nothing if you're not keeping any of it.

I've met plenty of HVAC business owners doing a million in revenue who are still living paycheck to paycheck. They're maxed out, stressed out, and wondering why they have nothing to show for all that growth.

On the flip side, I've met guys doing half that—$500,000 a year—but with higher profit margins, less stress, and actual financial freedom.

So, let me be clear: Revenue contests are pointless. Profit is the only number that matters.

A business doing $2 million in revenue but only keeping $100,000 after expenses is losing to the guy doing $750,000 in revenue with $250,000 in profit.

But you won't hear about that on social media. Why? Because "I made a million dollars" sounds better than "I actually took home $100,000."

But here's what matters:

- Can you pay your employees well and on time?
- Can you cover overhead without panic?
- Can you take a vacation without your business falling apart?
- Are you keeping more money at the end of the year than you started with?

That's the real flex.

Early on, I was just as guilty as anyone of chasing revenue for the sake of hitting bigger numbers. I wanted to hit that seven-figure mark because I thought that's what success looked like. But then reality smacked me in the face. I was working non-stop, hiring too fast, and underpricing my services, because I thought more jobs meant more success. But in reality, I was just spinning my wheels.

I had to shift my mindset. Instead of focusing on how much money was coming in, I started focusing on how much money I was keeping.

- I raised my prices to reflect the actual value I was providing.
- I cut unnecessary expenses that weren't driving real results.
- I stopped taking jobs that weren't profitable just to stay "busy."
- I built a company that worked for me, instead of me working for it.

And guess what? When I stopped chasing revenue and started focusing on profit, my business finally started to feel like success. This is why I designed this book: to teach you how to increase your actual profits by focusing on what improves profits in the fastest and most efficient ways.

Why Do Fast Wins Matter?

Business owners don't hire consultants to wait. They usually want immediate transformation. When I hired my first business coach ten years ago, I was struggling, and I didn't want a five-year plan. I needed money. I needed cash flow. I needed change—immediately. So that's how I structure my consulting.

When a home service business owner hires me, I like to prioritize the fastest wins that build momentum and generate cash flow as quickly as possible, because cash flow is what a business needs. Cash flow creates breathing room. Without it, a business will stay in survival mode, which is chaos.

Think of a cheetah chasing a gazelle. What is that gazelle doing? Is he thinking clearly? Absolutely not. He is in survival mode. That's chaos. That's how we normally run our businesses—because we jumped into business without a clear plan, and we're trying to hold it all together. But you can't operate or grow in survival mode, and cash flow calms things down. So, we want to get the quick wins as fast as possible to create space to address everything else.

What actually moves the needle? There are some core levers that you want to evaluate first. To make immediate change in the business—to completely turn it around in thirty days or less—there are a couple of things that need to be done.

One of those things is pricing. Underpricing kills profits faster than probably anything else. I mean, if you're charging less than what you're paying, then you're running a charity. I get it—we don't want to charge people more than what we think they should pay. But the fact is, the numbers tell you what you need to charge. Plain and simple.

Then there's sales. Changing conversion rates changes everything. If ten customers come into your business and you're priced correctly, but no one buys anything, then that's also a problem. So, it's not just pricing—it's also the sales process.

Community awareness matters too. If no one knows you exist, you can't sell anything. One thing I like to tell people is: If you went to your local store—your local Walmart or Target or wherever—and you stopped 100 people and asked them to name three businesses in your town that are the same type as yours, how many would name your business? What if you asked 1,000 people? How many would name yours? That's a pretty good indicator of where you are. People have to be aware of you in order to buy from you.

Being known is often better than being the best. Think of McDonald's. Is it the best food in the world? Definitely not. But it's the biggest restaurant chain in the world. I have competitors who aren't half as good as I am, but if people know them, they'll use them. So we need to make sure we are known so we get customers. We need to make sure our sales process is dialed in so we convert those customers. And we need to make sure we are priced correctly so that when we make sales, we actually make a profit.

You see this all the time—you just might not realize it. When you're driving down the road, you might pass 100 car dealerships, but you only notice the one with balloons flying on the cars. That's awareness. A small step—a couple of dollars for some balloons—but it makes a difference. That kind of thing changes a business.

So some common things that move the needle for a home service business in 30 days are the following:

- New pricing—an instant change with no extra effort.
- Calling your existing customers—almost instant results because you don't need to find new ones.
- Attending networking groups—a huge opportunity.

What doesn't matter—yet—is where business owners often invest. When businesses start, owners are excited and have a bit of extra cash to spend. So, one of the first things people do is go and make a logo. "Oh, I got my logo!" They're super excited about it. But making a logo doesn't bring in business, at least, not immediately. That comes later. What we're talking about here is what moves the needle right now.

"Oh, I got my website up." A website means nothing if no one knows you exist.

Trade businesses are especially bad for this. They start a business and immediately buy a whole bunch of tools. They'll get a shop, they'll get a building. This is the "getting a conference room when you don't even have employees" mentality—and you see that a lot. I know many small companies with just two employees and a massive shop. Why? Because they always wanted it.

But we don't want to make decisions early on that don't bring in cash flow. Every decision should bring in cash flow. And if you're reading this and you're strapped for cash, this is definitely for you.

Here's another thing businesses focus on at the beginning: digital marketing tactics with no real branding. We'll get into branding when I talk about irresistible identity in the messaging chapter.

We need to reframe our thinking. We don't want to focus on what we want as business owners. Instead, we must focus on what solves a problem for the customers we serve. That's how you make the biggest changes—quickly.

The Triage Process: Where to Start

Everything begins with asking powerful questions.

Step one: Relentlessly ask yourself, What's broken in my business? What's working—and what's not? Be brutally honest. This isn't the time to stroke our own egos.

Deep down, we already know what's broken. That's where we need to focus our attention.

Step two: Prioritize based on impact and speed of implementation, not based on "shiny object syndrome." Focus on the changes you can make quickly and effectively.

Take pricing, for example. It doesn't take much to adjust your pricing—it can be one of the fastest and most impactful changes you make. You can literally scratch out your old price, write a new one, and show it to someone today. Immediate action. We need to focus on changes that generate results the fastest.

Here's an example. I had a client we were doing sales training for. This client jumped from doing $100,000 in weekly sales to $200,000. That change—a full doubling of revenue—happened in just a fourteen-day period. How? All he did was shift his mindset to focus on building real connections with the customer.

One tiny behavior tweak resulted in a multiple six-figure gain per year for this business. My point is: whatever you can change the quickest— change that. Sometimes it's not something huge. It's something small. And yes, we can become overwhelmed. There are so many business books, so many speeches, so many TED Talks. But often, if we can just take one thing and say, "I can do that today—right now," then just do it. Take one thing and change it. Beware the trap of overcomplication. Most business owners avoid friction. But friction is often where the real progress begins.

I am the most guilty of this when it comes to certain things. I hate cold-calling people. I will do everything possible to avoid picking up the phone and calling someone cold.

Networking is often a similar issue. How many times have I heard some of my clients say, "Well, I don't want to go to a networking meeting because I'm an introvert"? Guess what? It doesn't matter what you are or what you're not—you have to do it. I have to cold call in my business, even though I don't like it.

Why? Because I need cash, and my business needs revenue. So, we have to push past things just because they create friction, just because they're uncomfortable or feel emotionally risky. We have to get past it.

I had an old business mentor. One day, I told him, "Hey, I'm having a hard time doing this in my business."

He turned around, looked at me, and said, "You'll get over it."

I asked, "What do you mean by that?"

And he said, "When your bills aren't paid, you'll start to cold call."

And that's a fact. We have to get past the things that are uncomfortable. But instead of facing discomfort, what business owners often do is chase shiny objects—things that feel productive but aren't—simply because they're easier.

Here's an analogy: Let's say someone's goal is to lose weight. The simplest way to lose weight is to eat less, move more, and drink more water. That's it. But while it's simple, it's not easy. So instead, we search for some magic mint leaf in the back of the Himalayan mountains that melts fat away. And we'll pay $300 for it online. Why? Because it's easier.

Oftentimes, the things that make the most difference are the hardest to do—but they bring about change the fastest. Real results can come quickly, but they require doing what's uncomfortable. Limiting beliefs often disguise themselves as logic. When we're faced with something difficult, one of the most common things I've heard clients say over my years of business consulting is: "That won't work in my city," or "I'm an introvert, so I can't network," or "You don't know my market."

All of those are psychological ways to keep us from doing the hard work. If it works in one city, it can work in another. A side note on that—when people say, "Well, that won't work in my market,"

I ask, "Can you think of a business in your market that you're competing against that is a really big company and grew really fast?"

Usually, they say, "Yeah."

And I say, "Hey, they're in your city,"

So, often, we make these excuses to avoid doing the emotionally risky things that make us uncomfortable.

Limiting beliefs from the owner of the business are always the ceiling of the business. Our emotional wiring from the past affects our present decision-making. That's a fact. Business minimalism means doing what works.

A lean and profitable business is focused, friction-tolerant, and nimble. Focused—not afraid of friction, not afraid of being uncomfortable, not afraid of doing things that make us feel nervous or that seem risky. Discipline is required to say no to the noise, say no to shiny object syndrome, and double down on the things that work—regardless of whether they scare us or not.

Conclusion: Get Back to the Basics

Forget fancy. Stop chasing the mint leaf on the other side of the Himalayan mountains. Focus on the things that serve your customer. Put your customer hat on and ask yourself: *If I were a customer of this business, what would I want?* Start solving that problem. Do it consistently. Do it now. You've now seen how focusing on the right levers—like quick wins, clarity, and community visibility—can create momentum and change the game fast. But if there's one lever that trumps them all in speed and impact, it's pricing.

Most business owners are undercharging—and don't even realize it. In the next chapter, we're going to fix that. It's time to stop guessing, start pricing with confidence, and finally earn what your service is worth.

Let's talk about profit—the kind that shows up in your bank account, not just on paper.

CHAPTER 3

Pricing for Profit:
Small Changes, Big Margins

Why does pricing come first? One day, while I was at a business event with some clients I was consulting, one of them stood up in front of everyone.

There were 300 people in the room, and he said, "I want to say thank you to my business coach, Michael Johnson, because we went from $500,000 a year to $1 million a year in our first six months of consulting." It really shocked me. I know the possibilities, but to hear someone say they went from half a million to a million in just six months of business consulting surprised me. But it was all because of one needle mover—the biggest thing that moves the needle the quickest, in my opinion—which is pricing.

Most businesses don't realize they're not making what they think they're making. Pricing is so emotionally charged for everyone that we often charge what we think we would pay—or what we think we should pay. But in reality, prices should not be based on what you think you should pay.

Prices should also not be based on what your competitor charges. Pricing must be based on your costs. It all depends on what you're spending in your business, and costs can be sneaky, because they can be hidden.

When I got my bachelor's degree in business, they called them "hidden costs." All that means is there are costs hiding from you—expenses you don't realize you're incurring, because you're not physically going into a store and buying those things. Here again, profit is the "relevance metric."

As we noted previously, the reality is that a business doing $2 million in revenue a year but only keeping $100,000 is losing to a company making just $750,000 a year but keeping $250,000. A lot of times, we focus on what are called "vanity metrics"—things we measure to boost our own ego. We might say, "I'm making $5 million a year in my business," or "I'm making $10 million a year." But that doesn't mean anything.

The only thing that matters is how much you're keeping. And how much you're keeping is dictated by how much you're charging—every single time you sell something. We work hard all day, every day, and we feel like we're making money. That was me in a nutshell for my first ten years in business. I was working twelve hours a day. I had a lot of customers. I was working super hard, coming home dirty, sweaty—and yet, I didn't have any money in the bank. I kept doing this for months and months.

I felt like I was making money, but I wasn't. I was experiencing what I call the "Swamped but Broke Phenomenon." There's an old saying that goes, "If you're going to be broke, why be tired at the same time?"

And the reason I wasn't making money was that—even though I was selling a lot, working a lot, and had a lot of customers—I was charging less than what I was paying in expenses because of hidden costs.

One of the biggest mistakes I made—and one of the most common issues I see when consulting businesses—is that we often set our prices based on our competitors or the market. For example, if we're selling candles and we see candles in a store being sold for $10, we might think, *Well, I can't sell mine for $11 because people will just go to Walmart and buy them for $10.* But it doesn't matter what Walmart is charging.

If Walmart is spending fifty cents to make a candle and you're spending $10, obviously, you can't compete with them. You have to price based on your cost and the margin you need to make. (We'll discuss margins in more detail later.)

Pricing errors typically come from either not knowing our true costs or pricing based on competitors. Both of these stem from a fear of losing customers. We tell ourselves things like, "Surely I can't charge this much for my service," because we feel uncomfortable. "Oh, I can't sell a candle for $100." But why not—if it's a better candle than the $10 one?

One example I give is the tale of two customers. When we feel uneasy about pricing something a certain way, just look around. You'll see someone wearing a $10 watch—and right next to them, someone wearing a $12,000 watch. People buy what they want. If someone sees the value in what you sell, they'll buy it. If they don't, they won't. Simple as that. So we have to price based on value and cost, not on emotions like, *Oh my gosh, if I charge this price, no one's going to buy. I'll lose customers. The sky will fall. I'll lose everything.* We have to set emotions aside and understand our numbers.

Let me give you an example: A company making $600,000 a year with $300,000 in expenses might think they're doing great—but they won't know their true net margins until their overhead is properly calculated.

I had a client I was coaching who came to me making $4 million a year. I asked, "How are you doing?"

The client replied, "We're doing really well. We're making a lot of money."

"Okay, how much money are you keeping at the end of the year?" I asked.

"I'm not sure, but I know we're doing good," they responded. So we pulled their profit and loss statement.

They were losing money—every year. They were running at a negative $110,000 annually. They weren't doing well at all. They were underpriced.

Now, what if they raised their prices, lost a bunch of customers, went from $4 million to $2 million in revenue, but kept $300,000? Would they be in a better position? Absolutely. It's okay to lose customers if you raise your prices. It's actually better to have fewer customers paying more than to keep low prices, win every bid, serve everyone, and lose money.

Raising prices is the fastest lever in business. It can be done instantly. That's why I love it. That's why I often focus on pricing on day one when I start consulting with businesses. Because we can do it the *same* day—it doesn't require a long process to figure out.

We don't have to create a system, build a process, hire employees, and do all of that. Really, you can just flip the switch and say, "This is the price now." I mean, think about it—when you walk into a restaurant, they hand you the menu. It has the prices printed on it. But they could have changed those prices just five minutes ago. You wouldn't know. That's the beauty of it—pricing can be changed quickly.

No big production. No extra work. But what's the impact? The impact is an immediate increase in margins. When you raise your prices, you need fewer customers to make the same amount of money. And like I've said before, pricing is often tied to personal insecurity.

Many business owners project their own budget mindset onto their customers. You see this a lot in sales. I remember one day my wife wanted to buy a new vehicle—one she had always dreamed of. We didn't grow up with money. We came from a tough neighborhood. And even after becoming financially free, we still felt guilty about spending a certain amount. She wanted this vehicle, and it cost $50,000.

I said, "Babe, you deserve it. You hardly ever spend anything on yourself. You can afford it. Let's go buy it."

So we went to the dealership. We walk onto the lot, and the salesman comes up and asks, "How can I help you?"

I told him, "That vehicle over there—I want it."

And the first thing he said was, "Oh man, that's like $50,000. Are you sure you don't want this one instead?"

See what happened? Every person has an emotional connection to what's "a lot" and what's "not a lot." But that kind of emotional projection doesn't belong in sales—and it definitely doesn't belong in business. We have to let go of the fear of losing bids or losing customers to lower-priced competitors.

In fact, we should be okay with losing some customers—especially the ones who are only focused on price. If we started our business with the dream of offering the best possible product, then we shouldn't compromise that by trying to please everyone. I know I'm the best business in my market. I charge more because I'm the best. I don't necessarily want a person who only cares about price.

I remember my fear the first time I raised my prices. My first thought was, *No one will pay me this.* Where was that coming from? It was a self-limiting belief. Somewhere deep down, I didn't believe I deserved to be paid that much. But why not? My business coach told me, "Why don't you just try it? You can always change it. If no one pays it, you can go back. What do you really have to lose?" So I took his advice. I changed my prices instantly—almost tripled them in one day.

And no one skipped a beat. Not a single customer even questioned it—because the truth is, most of your customers already know you're too cheap. They've been waiting for you to raise your prices. They're just hoping you don't figure it out soon.

The only one who doesn't realize you're underpriced—most of the time—is you, the business owner. That's because you're pricing based on emotions or your competitors, without truly knowing your actual costs. And that's exactly what we're going to dive into. We don't want to project our own budget mindset onto our customers.

There's a saying: "selling out of your wallet," or "selling out of your budget." But we don't sell based on our budget—we sell for a margin. Often, we're afraid of losing sales to lower-cost competitors. And that fear just keeps building. So we need to reframe our thinking and understand that price increases are reversible.

If that idea helps take the fear out of it for you—try it, measure it, and adjust. One thing I teach people is this: if you're too scared to raise your prices and risk rocking the boat, how about keeping prices the same—for now—for your existing customers? And when a new customer comes in, give them the new price and see what happens.

Check your closing rate. If ten people come in and zero people buy, it might not even be a pricing issue. That might be a sales issue, but let's not get ahead of ourselves. Let's first look at the common pricing mistakes.

Pricing Based on Competitors

Never price your products or services based on what your competitors are charging. Why? Because you don't know anything about their financial health.

Businesses go out of business every day. You've seen it happen. I even shared a story about a company making $4 million in revenue but netting a loss of $100,000 per year.

Do you really want to copy their pricing? No—you don't want to go out of business with them. That's what we call a race to the bottom.

Pricing Based on Gut Feelings Instead of Cost-Margin Formulas

Saying, "I think something like this should cost around this much," is not a strategy. The problem is that everyone has a different idea of what things should cost, and most of them are wrong. As the saying goes: "Men lie, women lie, but numbers never lie." That's why we base pricing on real costs and target margins, not on instinct.

Discounting by Default

Running discounts just because you think it will boost sales? Or undercutting other businesses as a competitive strategy? That's the old *I'll price match that guy* mindset.

But why are you doing that? Is it helping your bottom line—or just devaluing your offer?

Misunderstanding Value

If your business offers more—faster service, a better customer experience, a compelling story—then you're creating more value. And when you deliver more value, you're justified in charging more. Your price should reflect not just what you do, but how well you do it and the experience you deliver.

We see this everywhere. Starbucks coffee is $6. McDonald's coffee is $0.99. What's the difference? People feel better about one over the other. So they go there and pay more—willingly.

If you offer something people want, they will pay more. People don't buy based on price. They really don't. People buy based on emotion, as the earlier example of the watches illustrated.

Just don't be afraid to be the higher-priced option. Let me share a personal story that really helped me understand this. I went to a job site to sell someone a new heating and air conditioning system.

At the time, I really needed the job to close. I needed the money badly. So I thought, *I'm going to lower my price—really low—just to make sure I get this job and can pay my bills.* I competed on price, but the guy didn't buy on the spot.

I called him the next day and asked, "Hey, when would you like me to start the job?"

He said, "Oh, the other company did it yesterday."

I was so disappointed because I knew I had the lowest price. So I asked him, "Can I ask—what made you go with the other company?"

He said, "Well, they offered *(this, this, this, this, and this)*."

And I said, "Oh man, I could have offered that too."

He replied, "Yeah, I know—but you didn't."

Then I asked him, "How much did they charge you?" Turns out, the other company was $2,000 more than I was.

That moment completely reframed my mindset. It proved to me that people don't just buy based on who's the cheapest. So get that fear out of your mind. Charge what you need to charge—to cover your bills, meet your expenses, and make a profit.

This is the value-based pricing philosophy. We need to price according to the value delivered, not the number of hours worked. That's the mindset shift from employee to business owner.

My dad was an electrician. He worked at a hospital for thirty-six years. If he wanted to make more money in a month, he had to work more hours. If he worked fewer hours, he made less. I carried that same mindset into my own business at first. If I needed more money, I'd just work more. I didn't realize that the value I was delivering was what actually mattered.

Here's an example: If someone's home is 100 degrees—and I can get it down to 72 degrees tonight—that's worth more than the competitor who can't come out for two weeks. That is value. And we need to price accordingly. If you're a plumber, it's the same thing.

If you own a bakery, it's the same thing. Customers often associate higher prices with professionalism and trust.

But here's the key: You cannot charge higher prices and offer worse service. That's a recipe for disaster. You'll go out of business very quickly that way.

However, if you offer a better service and charge a higher price, there is absolutely a customer for you. I raised my hourly rate from $75 to $300 in one day, and received no resistance at all.

Let me tell you another story. One day, I was on a job site. We had just completed a job that totaled several thousand dollars. When it was time for the homeowner to pay, he went upstairs, came down, reached into his bag, and started counting out hundred-dollar bills—one by one—right into my hand. At this time, our team looked good. We had our vans professionally wrapped, with signage all over. Everyone on my team was in uniform. We wore boot covers inside the house.

Right after, another company pulled up, and their van looked like it had just driven out of Hades. It was the worst van you've ever seen—dented, paint peeling, banged up. The guys had cigarettes in their hands. They came out and diagnosed a plumbing issue—because we were doing the heating and cooling work—and they said to the homeowner, "Hey, we can fix your plumbing for a hundred bucks."

Keep in mind, this guy had water spraying everywhere under his house. It was a disaster. And yet, the homeowner declined their $100 repair offer. He said he didn't have the money, while counting out thousands of dollars to me. What does that tell you? It tells you he didn't value that company—their image, their presentation. So here's the takeaway: If we create more value, deliver more trust, look more professional, and perform better, we can charge more.

People will pay more. They'll pay less if they don't feel trust—if they don't view you as a professional, because people don't buy based on price. They buy based on emotion. Wrapped vans, uniforms, branding—everything along the customer journey—supports your pricing. Believe it or not, simply answering the phone on the first ring is incredibly powerful.

We've talked about the tale of two customers. We won't go into that here, but consider the strategy: new customers get new prices, while existing customers keep their legacy rates—at least initially. Think of it as a test. If you're hesitant to raise prices across the board, try implementing the new pricing only for new customers and observe their reactions. They don't know you. They don't know anything about you. So, observe how they react, and then gradually introduce those prices to your existing customers.

Now, let's talk about the pricing strategy process.

The Pricing Strategy Process

The first step is to audit your costs and run your pricing math. These are the foundational tasks you must complete when setting your prices.

Number one, you need to understand your true expenses—not just the ones you think you have, but the actual costs that show up every time you check your bank account. Every swipe of your card represents a real expense, whether you want to acknowledge it or not. You need to be honest about what it truly costs to run your business. Next, consider this: what margins do you need to hit your goals? For those who may not have a deep understanding of pricing, let me explain. When we talk about margins, we're talking about how much money is left after expenses, and how that contributes to your profit. There are a few ways to make money in this world:

1. You can work a job—trade an hour of your time for a fixed amount of money.
2. You can put your money into a savings account, which typically yields less than 1% interest.
3. You can invest in the stock market, which, on average, might give you a 6% annual return.

And then there's being in business—another powerful way to generate income, often with much greater potential, but it requires careful strategy and pricing to be profitable.

So, you have to ask yourself: *What percentage return do I want on the money I invest in my business?* In a nine-to-five job, it's easy—you ask how much you want to earn per hour. But in business, you're investing money to make more money. So the question becomes: *How much do I want back for every dollar I spend?* That's what we call a margin. For example, if I spend $100, and I want to make $30 in profit, that's a 30% profit margin.

If you want to make 50% of that $100 you spent, that would be a 50% profit margin. These are the questions you have to ask yourself: Where do your current prices even come from? Most businesses have no clue.

And I like to see the confusion sometimes, because it kind of shocks consulting clients into, you know, realizing what we're doing. Like, *Hey, this is a real consultation. This is different.* This is a reframe.

I'll say, "How did you come up with your prices?" And normally, they'll say, "What do you mean?" I repeat, "How did you come up with your prices?" And they say, "I don't really know." And that is 99% of business owners. I was there. And there's no shame in that. The truth is, none of us were born business owners. No person is born a business owner. You're born a baby, not a business owner.

So, to start with pricing, we need better branding and stronger messaging. We need added service elements. Are we faster? Are we better? Are we more efficient? Whatever it is. Using trust signals is another way. Did you win any awards? Or, if you own a barbecue truck, did you win any barbecue competitions? Put those on the sides of the truck.

You can sell a piece of barbecue for a dollar more if you won the North Carolina Barbecue Competition. People are going to say, "Ooh, I would spend a dollar more for that." So: trust signals, awards, longevity in business.

One thing I always say in my business messaging is: "We've been in business for over twenty years. We have over 800 five-star reviews." So when people hear our prices, they're okay with it, because I've built trust.

You have trust signals, too. Maybe you don't realize it. That's why I'm adding the chapter on branding—because I'm going to teach you how to create a message that commands a better price.

Here are two signs that it's time to increase your prices. One, your schedule is overwhelming. You're working an insane amount. You have a lot of customers, but the amount in the bank literally does not grow. Like, it literally doesn't grow. You had $1,000 in the bank in January, and in March, you have $500, even though tons of customers are coming in. That's a sign your prices are too low.

Two, you have a very high closing rate. That could mean you're not charging enough. What does that mean—high closing rate? A thousand people came into your store, and a thousand people bought that cupcake. That probably means you have a little room to raise your prices.

I told you about the client who went from half a million dollars a year to a million dollars, with just one change: raising his prices. It was day one, episode one. The thing we did on the very first day made the biggest difference.

I also told you my story—that I was the low-price leader. When I made my first coupon after starting my business, I didn't hire a digital artist. I had no idea what I was doing. I just opened a Word document and typed: *"Lowest prices in town."* I'm embarrassed to even mention this. It had a logo that looked like a little kid made it. I printed out 100 copies and passed them around. No wonder I was working hard but not making any money.

If you're the owner of a business and you're passionate about what you do, there's a pretty good chance you're better than the big corporate stores. If you own a small coffee shop, you probably make a better cup of coffee than the big corporate monster everyone goes to. So why charge less than them if your coffee's better? That's where the mindset shift around money begins.

Here are some common limiting beliefs:

- "My customers can't afford it." Sure they can. People buy what they want to buy.

- "No one in my area pays that much." We know that one's a lie—because there's a big competitor in your city who charges way more than you do.
- "If I charge more, I'll lose everyone." The truth is, you'll lose some. You won't lose everyone. And losing customers is okay—especially if they're the ones paying too little for your services. So let's reframe that. Instead of saying, "My customers can't afford it," say, "Well, I'm not my customer. Maybe I can't afford it—but that doesn't mean they can't."

High-end buyers exist in every industry. In every industry, no matter what business you're in, there are people who want to spend a lot on your product, and people who want to spend very little. Let's focus on the high-end buyers—not the cheap buyers.

Here's another reframe: Fewer customers at higher prices means more margin and less stress. If I can make the same amount of money with three customers as I can with ten customers at a cheaper price—and I don't have to run around solving problems for those ten—I can just focus on those three. That means I'm working less and stressing less.

Pricing confidence is a reflection of self-worth. That's a fact. So if you're having a hard time raising prices, I want you to focus on two things:

Really get to know your numbers. Ask yourself: *Why are you so scared to charge more?*

Is it because you don't believe you're worth it? That's something we need to dig into—because it won't just affect your business, it'll affect your life in many different ways. The ripple effect of better pricing.

It will affect sales. It'll be a lot easier to hit big goals with fewer transactions. It'll affect your marketing.

Higher prices allow you to buy more ads. The more money you make, the more you can afford that huge billboard or that TV commercial to compete with the big guys. You'll never be able to afford it if you're not making any money. If you're a negative $100,000 company, you'll never be able to buy ads.

It also helps your operations. There's less strain on your team because they don't have to do as much all day. And there are more resources to give back to your team. You can pay them more. You can give them bonuses. You can give them more time off.

It also affects customer quality. Higher prices attract more serious, respectful clients. It marks a shift from cash-flow survival to margin-based growth.

This is what price changes do. And it's such an easy lever. It's as simple as flipping a light switch. Really, all you have to do is just tell people: "This is how much it costs." That's literally all it takes to change it.

Conclusion: Raise to Rise

Pricing is the easiest lever to pull with the biggest reward. Confidence, clarity, and simple math can lead to a business transformation. So the thing that made me shift my pricing was basically pure necessity. I remember thinking, *Okay, I have a wife*. And at the time, I had two children. I have three now. I remember looking at my two sons and thinking: *They're going to grow up. I'm working incredibly hard. And by the time they're grown, I'll probably have worked forty or fifty years, and I won't have anything to give them. And that's a shame. They'll be able to tell stories like, "Dad owned a business. His business was known in town. He worked on tens of thousands of houses."* But there would be no money to leave them. That really got to me emotionally. And then, looking at my wife—she's just so loving, so patient, and always so supportive— I thought, *Man, I'm not leaving anything.*

Our bills were a struggle, all because I was scared to charge a certain amount of money. And I felt like I was bigger than that.

So I remember thinking: *If I don't leave my kids an inheritance, if I don't pay the bills or become a financial strength in my family, it's not going to be because I was scared to charge what I'm worth. If I fall short, let it be for another reason—not fear.* That moment shifted me. I knew I had to get past my own emotions about money—what I saw my dad do, what I saw my mom do, what I experienced growing up in my neighborhood and in my culture.

And I said, "You know what? Forget all of that. I'm not going to let something as small as fear or emotional baggage tied to money stop me from leaving an inheritance, or from passing my business on to my children."

I've created a video for you to help you price
your services accurately and quickly.

Scan the QR code:

CHAPTER 4

Why Service Plans Are the Backbone of an HVAC Business

Imagine having a magic ATM that deposits money into your account every month, without you having to do anything extra. That's what service plans can be for your HVAC business. They're not just another offering—they're the backbone of your company's cash flow, stability, and future growth.

When you build a strong foundation of service plans, you're creating recurring revenue that covers your bills, funds your team, and cushions your business during slow seasons. Every plan you sell is like planting a seed that grows into consistent income and long-term customer loyalty.

The Power of Predictable Cash Flow

Imagine this: You start January 1st already knowing you have $300,000 coming in throughout the year from service plan renewals alone. That's revenue you can count on—no guessing, no scrambling to make ends meet.

Here's a simple breakdown:

- If you sell 500 service plans at $240/year, that's $120,000 annually.
- Divide that by 12 months, and you're bringing in $10,000 every single month—before you even book a single emergency repair or installation job.

This steady income covers your fixed expenses—rent, payroll, supplies—making everything else pure profit. And that's just the beginning.

Real-world example: One HVAC company started selling service plans five years ago. Now, they collect over $25,000 every month before running any new calls. During slower months, like January or February, they don't worry about how to keep their team busy or cover the bills—the service plan revenue takes care of it.

Service plans increase your company's value. Thinking of selling your business one day? Here's the first question a buyer will ask:

"How many active service plans do you have?"

Why? Because service plans show your business has loyal, recurring customers and predictable income. It's like showing a steady heartbeat that proves your company is healthy and viable. Businesses with robust service plan memberships sell for higher prices because they come with built-in revenue streams.

Growing Revenue from Repeat Customers

Customers with service plans spend more money—period. Why? Because they trust your company. They're more likely to:

- Approve repairs when you suggest them
- Upgrade their systems with you when the time comes
- Purchase add-ons like UV lights, air purifiers, or surge protectors

Think of it this way: If each service plan customer spends an extra $500 on additional services each year, and you have 500 members, that's an extra $250,000 annually—all from customers who are already loyal to your business.

Building Long-Term Relationships Equals More Profit

Service plans turn one-time customers into lifelong clients. When customers feel cared for, they stop shopping around. They'll call you first because they know you're reliable and trustworthy. They're not just clients—they're part of your HVAC family.

Real-world example: An HVAC business with over 2,000 active service plan members noticed a powerful trend: every time they sent out seasonal reminders, their phones lit up with new calls—not just for maintenance, but for extra services and installations. Thanks to service plans, their team stayed busy year-round.

Protecting Against Seasonal Slumps

Slow seasons can be stressful. But with a steady stream of service plans, you won't panic when demand dips. Those recurring payments will help cover:

- Payroll
- Rent and utilities
- Marketing efforts to generate more business

Instead of worrying about how to stay afloat during the off-season, you can focus on growth, training, and strategic planning.

Unlocking a Profitable Sales Cycle

Service plans aren't just about cash flow—they set the stage for future sales.

Here's how it works:

1. A customer signs up for your plan.
2. They trust you because of regular contact and consistent service.
3. When their system starts aging, guess who they call? You.
4. You handle the replacement, and because they're loyal, you're not competing against other bids.

This cycle keeps customers with your business for years, driving revenue without constant advertising.

How to Track and Grow Your Service Plan Revenue

To maximize the power of service plans, you need to track them effectively. Use tools like Housecall Pro or Breezy to:

- Monitor how many active members you have
- See when renewals are due
- Send reminders automatically

Tracking lets you see the true health of your HVAC business at a glance—and helps ensure that no opportunity slips through the cracks.

Set Goals to Supercharge Your Revenue

Here's a powerful strategy: Cover your monthly overhead with service plans alone.

Example:

- Monthly expenses: $20,000
- Service plan income per customer: $240/year
- To cover overhead, you'd need roughly 1,000 service plan members

Once your overhead is covered, every repair, installation, or upsell becomes pure profit.

The Backbone of Your Business

Think of service plans like the foundation of a house—you can't build a strong structure without them. They provide:

- Steady, predictable cash flow to cover your bills and fund your growth
- Higher business value for when you're ready to sell
- Customer loyalty that drives additional sales and long-term revenue
- Protection during slow seasons to keep your business thriving year-round

Start today. Every service plan you sell brings you one step closer to predictable income, financial freedom, and a future-proof HVAC business that runs like a well-oiled machine.

How to Create and Structure Service Plans

Imagine you're building a LEGO castle. You wouldn't start by throwing bricks everywhere—you'd follow a plan. A solid service plan works the same way. You need a clear blueprint to help customers keep their HVAC systems running like clockwork—and to keep your business thriving.

Simplify your plan tiers. Think of it like choosing ice cream sizes:

- **Bronze Plan:** This is like getting a single scoop—just one simple, no-frills annual maintenance visit. It's a basic check-up for customers who want a little care without the extras.

- **Silver Plan:** Think of this as a double scoop—two visits per year, spring and fall. Customers also get priority scheduling, meaning they jump ahead in line when they need service.

- **Gold Plan:** This is the triple scoop with all the toppings—two visits per year, priority scheduling, 10% discounts on repairs, waived diagnostic fees, and small, thoughtful gifts upon renewal, like a surprise thank-you package or branded goodies.

Real-world example: One HVAC company added a perk where, for every year a customer stayed on the plan, they earned $100 toward a new system. After ten years, that's $1,000 off a brand-new HVAC setup! Customers loved it because it made staying loyal feel rewarding, and it kept them around for the long haul.

Add Value Beyond the Basics

Imagine sending a small package of flower seeds in the spring with a note that says, "Thanks for growing with us." Or a custom pizza cutter in the fall, because nothing says "we appreciate you" like pizza night. These thoughtful touches make customers feel valued—and keep them coming back.

Launch Quickly and Improve Later

Just like riding a bike—you don't need to master every detail before you start pedaling. Launch your service plan now, even if it's basic. You can always add perks later, like priority service or discounts, as your business grows.

How to Sell Maintenance Plans Effectively

Selling isn't about being pushy—it's about being a helpful guide. Imagine you're helping someone navigate a maze. You're there to show them the easiest, safest path.

Proactive Selling at Every Touchpoint

- **First Contact:** Teach your office staff to mention service plans as soon as someone calls. For example: "Hey, did you know we have a membership that saves you money and gives you priority service?"

- **On-Site Touchpoint:** When technicians are with customers, they should highlight plan benefits naturally. "You know, joining our plan today could save you money on this repair."

- **Post-Service Follow-Up:** Use automated systems to send a friendly thank-you message and remind customers of the benefits of joining.

Relatable Selling Points

- "Your air conditioner works harder than your car. Would you skip oil changes on your car?"
- "Did you know your AC is probably the most expensive appliance in your home? Our plan helps protect that investment."

Story Example:

A technician once told a customer, "Imagine if your AC breaks on the hottest day of summer and every company says they can't get to you for two weeks. With our plan, we guarantee priority service—you'll be first in line." The customer signed up on the spot.

Overcome Objections by Making It Simple

- Too Expensive? "It's just $24 a month—that's less than Netflix, but it could save you thousands on repairs."
- I'll Call If It Breaks: "Most breakdowns happen without warning—and they're expensive. This plan helps you avoid those big surprise bills."

How to Spiff Your Team for Maximum Sales

Think of spiffs like giving gold stars at school—they're small rewards that make people feel appreciated and motivated.

Spiff Structure (Make It Rewarding):

- $20 bonus for every plan sold
- $10 bonus when the same customer renews
- Extra rewards for upselling accessories—like a $10 bonus for every UV light sold.
- Dispatcher Incentives: Dispatchers are the first point of contact with customers. Offer them the same rewards as technicians for every plan they sell over the phone.
- Recognition Programs: Give out "Top Seller of the Month" awards.
- Offer prizes like gift cards or an extra day off for hitting sales milestones.

Track and Celebrate Success

Create a fun leaderboard and update it weekly. Recognize achievements with shout-outs during team meetings.

One company noticed that after introducing a leaderboard and monthly bonuses, their service plan sales doubled in just three months. Employees started competing—friendly competition drove motivation through the roof.

Marketing and Promotion Tactics

Marketing is like throwing a party—you want to invite everyone early so they're excited before the fun starts.

Advertise Early:

- Run ads for spring maintenance as early as February. Be the first company on your customers' radar so that when competitors show up later, you've already secured the business.

Creative Promotions:

- Run a Valentine's Day special offering discounted rates for signups in February
- Offer new customers a free maintenance visit one year after installation—this gets you back in their home and keeps the relationship strong

Use Your Existing Customers:

- Send email and text reminders with limited-time offers
- Share social media posts showing before-and-after photos of dirty coils and clean systems—visual proof that your service works

Conclusion

Imagine waking up every month to see thousands of dollars automatically deposited from service plans. That's the power of a well-structured maintenance program. The best part? It builds long-term loyalty, boosts your revenue, and keeps your team motivated.

Start small. Sell one plan today. Get your team excited with spiffs. Share customer stories. Before long, you'll build a loyal customer base and a strong, profitable business that practically runs itself. Pricing gets you in the game. But sales? Sales are how you win. The right price means nothing if your team can't book the call, overcome objections, or close the deal. That's why this next chapter is all about conversions—what happens between the moment a lead reaches out and when they say yes. We'll look at the scripts, mindset, and process you need to turn more opportunities into booked, profitable jobs.

CHAPTER 5

Sales That Convert

"Sales" is a bad word to a lot of people. The moment you start talking about making more sales, increasing revenue, or closing deals, it tends to make people uncomfortable. Many see it as sleazy or equate it with selling out.

There are a lot of mental roadblocks that come up when discussing sales. But here's something I always say: "Sales is serving. Sales is not about manipulation."

All sales are service. What do I mean by that? Think about it. If you reframe sales in your mind, you'll realize that when you're talking to a customer, it's usually because they have a problem that needs solving—unless you're just cold calling, of course.

But most of the time—especially in the trades like plumbing, HVAC, or electrical—you're in someone's home because they invited you. They had a problem, and they called you to fix it. You're not intruding or pushing something they don't want. You're there to help.

Here's a great analogy my sales partner, Ariel Robinson, often uses: Sales is like being a doctor. When you go to the doctor, you're being sold—big time. You might not realize it, but it's happening. The doctor prescribes medication, bills your insurance, suggests treatments—but you never feel like you're being sold to.

Why? Because the doctor isn't pitching you anything. They're diagnosing. And how do they diagnose? By asking questions.

We'll get to that in a minute. But first, let's tackle one big issue: Sales is not sleazy. That mindset? I call it head trash. We need to take out the trash—the negative beliefs like, "I need revenue in my business, but I don't want to be a salesperson." That's head trash. And trash belongs in the trash can, not in your head. Let's throw out those limiting beliefs. Get rid of that old idea of sales so we can move forward, and I can teach you how to sell effectively and with integrity.

Now, let's talk practically. If a customer is still talking to you—if they didn't hang up, walk out of your store, or kick you out of their house during a plumbing estimate—they have a problem and are open to help. You are the doctor in this scenario.

And just like a doctor, you don't "sell" by pushing something they don't need. You sell by diagnosing. Think about the last time you visited a doctor. You had some sort of pain or discomfort. And what did the doctor do? They asked question after question.

- Where is the pain?
- On a scale of 1 to 10, how bad is it? Is it throbbing or sharp?
- When did it start? Does it happen all the time?

You answered, giving more and more information. That's exactly how effective sales conversations should go.

And then, after that conversation, the doctor says, "Okay, based on our talk, I think you need to take this medicine." And you gladly take it without question, even though you were being sold that medicine. That's because the doctor is serving you, not pitching to you.

So let's reframe our mindset and acknowledge this: you have to sell to make revenue—period. And people will buy from you if you convince them.

But the scary thing for a lot of people is that customers are usually thinking only about dollar signs. They're afraid. When you ring their doorbell to give them an air conditioning estimate, you hear "ding-dong"—but they hear dollar signs. They hear "cha-ching." They're nervous. They're afraid. And they're not just going to buy right away. You have to convince them they're making the right decision. And that's what sales is. If you can't do that—or if you're scared to do it, or feel like it makes you a sellout—then your revenue won't be enough.

And of course, revenue is oxygen to a business. So let's start with this foundation: selling is serving.

Now, most salespeople don't actually sell, right? If we replace the word "sell" with "serve," we'll see that most salespeople don't serve their clients. They pitch. And that's a huge mistake, because pitching doesn't convert. It doesn't uncover what someone actually wants or needs. All pitching does is focus on what we want and need: "I want to sell this to you for this amount, so I'm going to tell you everything about it and hope you'll buy it—whether you need it or not."

That's not serving. That's selfish. In a sense, that is sleazy. But selling in a serving way is effective. So we need to stop pitching—because it doesn't work. We need to find what someone already wants and needs.

That's the reason they called you in the first place. Once you discover what they want and need, you simply give it to them. That's not even a sales transaction — it's a friendly exchange.

"Oh, you need this? I have one."

"Sure, I'd love to buy it!"

So, we're going to reframe sales as making helpful, relevant offers. Sales as service — a personal approach.

Selling is about understanding someone's needs and giving them a solution. That's all it is. We're shifting from pitching to serving — and I'm going to show you exactly how to do that.

The first step is to figure out what people want. The way to do that is to ask three or four questions — at minimum — until you fully understand what their real need is. This approach works not only in business, but also in your relationships. It makes them richer. Why? Because most people give a surface-level answer to the first question you ask. A perfect example? When you ask someone, "Hey, how are you doing?" They're going to say, "Good." They didn't even think about it. It's just a knee-jerk response.

But when you ask the second question — "How are you really doing?" — now we're starting to get somewhere. It's usually not the first question that uncovers someone's real need. It's the second, the third, the fourth, the fifth, the sixth. So let's get comfortable in our sales—or service—roles with asking question, after question, after question.

And remember: people want to talk about themselves. During the sales process, don't get flustered if someone says no. Just keep asking questions. People literally come into your business with a problem. They want to talk about it because they want someone to understand the pain they're feeling.

How frustrating is it when you call tech support? Your phone isn't working—it has no signal. You call tech support. But no one's really listening. They just send you back and forth between departments, and your issue goes unresolved for one simple reason: they didn't listen. Don't you want to tell the tech support person exactly what the problem is? Wouldn't they be able to help more if they actually listened and asked more questions? We've all been on that side of sales so many times. So when we're on the selling side, it's the same thing.

We can use our own experiences and frustrations as buyers to better understand how our customers feel. People want to talk about themselves. They want to talk about the problem they're having. They want to explain it so that someone (you) can help them solve it. Understanding this gives you a huge advantage.

So, lesson number one is to ask as many questions as possible. Think about the doctor example I just shared. How much better is the diagnosis when the patient gives a detailed explanation? Where the pain is. How often it happens. What time of day it occurs. Whether it happens after eating this but not after eating that, the patient has basically done the work for the doctor.

It's the same when we're trying to close a deal.

Let's say you own an electrical company, and someone asks for an estimate to rewire their house. Of course, you could just walk in and say, "That'll be $10,000." Or you could start asking questions:

- "What's the reason you want your house rewired?"
- "Oh, the lights are blinking in the bedroom?"
- "Interesting—when did that start?"
- "After the lightning storm?"
- "Is it happening all the time?"

You dig down to the root of the problem. Then you can say, "Based on what you're describing, not only do you need a full house rewire, but you also need a surge protector to prevent this from happening again, especially since we get so many lightning storms each year." Now you've just upsold—without selling something they don't need.

Remember, based on this example, you're taking the information they give you and offering them something they actually need. You're more likely to close deals that way because you're meeting them at their point of need. This also helps you present things clearly and confidently.

The better you understand your customer, the more confident you become in offering solutions. And let's face it—human beings are incredibly skilled at reading nonverbal cues. In fact, 90% of our interactions with others are nonverbal. If you're not confident in what you're offering, then the customer won't feel confident about buying it from you. But when you truly develop a deep understanding of what they need, you become confident that what you're offering will solve their problem. And that kind of pure confidence instills trust and gives them the confidence to buy from you. So I hope you're following what I'm saying.

What makes a sales process effective? Here are some non-negotiables.

Ask Deep, Relevant Questions

And not just one question—ask many. It's an age-old saying, almost a cliché at this point. When you walk into a business, someone usually says, "Hey, hello, how can I help you today?" There's a reason it's so common: it works. They're asking you directly what you need so they can offer exactly what you came in for. It's simple, but it's brilliant.

If you can ask the right questions and find out exactly what your customer wants to buy, then you can present exactly that. If you don't, you're throwing darts in the dark, presenting products or services they may not care about. No wonder your close rate is low.

So—ask questions. Ask lots of them.

Don't Be a Robot—Build Rapport Early and Often

People don't buy from cold robots. They buy from people they trust and feel a connection with. So what is rapport? It's simply making a personal, friendly connection.

I had a conversation with my team today during our morning meeting. They asked me, "What's the first thing you do when giving a bid or estimate to a customer?" My answer might surprise you: I focus on building a connection before I talk about price or what we offer.

When someone answers the door, I say, "Good morning!"—a small, conventional gesture that's powerful because it's familiar and warm. Then, I'll look for something to comment on—maybe a license plate from Georgia or Florida—and bring that up naturally. But remember: don't make things up. People can spot insincerity from a mile away. If there's nothing personal to comment on, don't force it. Sales is about serving. If you're dishonest, you're not serving at all.

You want your customer to feel like you're that trusted uncle, brother, or sister giving them solid, honest advice. Imagine this: your brother calls and says, "Hey, I'm going to buy a car tomorrow. Any advice before I go?" How would you talk to him? That's the same energy and authenticity you should bring to your real customers. Be a trusted advisor—that's what people want.

Present Tailored Options

This is another non-negotiable. Present options tailored to the client's needs. I like to call it a "menu"—a concept I picked up from my sales and business coaching partner, Ariel Robinson.

Think of it like this: how successful would a restaurant be if it only served one dish? Sure, a few people might love it, but most customers wouldn't find it appealing. That's why restaurants hand you a menu. The waiters (or servers, quite literally) are selling, but they're doing it in a service-oriented way. They don't just say, "Here's the steak we want you to buy." Instead, they give you options and let you choose.

In sales, your job is to do the same. If you're only presenting one option that isn't tailored to what the client actually wants, you'll lose a lot of people. Ask deep questions (remember point #1), learn about their needs, and then present a range of options that address those needs.

If you've asked ten to twelve insightful questions, you'll have a good understanding of what they want. From there, present four to five well-aligned solutions. Give them a "menu" they can choose from, and make it easy for them to say yes.

Always, Always, Always Close in Person

This one is simple: always close in person when possible. Think about restaurants again—they're closing the deal in person because you're hungry and you're eating right then and there.

But let's talk about the trades, because I'm a business mentor in that space. I coach professionals in plumbing, HVAC, electrical, lawn care, home service businesses like these. For these types of businesses, we typically do estimates in person, right at the client's home.

But what I've seen all too often in my years of coaching is this: we show up, ask the right questions, the customer tells us what they need, we offer some options…and then we say, "Hey, I'll head back to the office, put together a quote, and email it to you." That is a huge, huge, *huge* no-no. Never just send a quote later.

Never do it. You must present the options in person, because that's when you ask for the sale. This requires a complete reframing of how we think about quoting.

We talked about reframing our thoughts, and that includes reframing the idea that it's ever okay to send estimates later. This is a huge issue.

In fact, it's almost like an epidemic in the home service industry. You call someone to cut your grass or build a deck, and what happens? They show up… but never send the quote. Always close in person.

You're already there—so why not just ask for the sale? I've seen the closing rate for my heating and air conditioning company skyrocket simply by asking, "Would you like to schedule the job right now?"

A huge number of people say, "Let's do it," just because I asked. Now, think about this: when I say, "I'll head back to the office and send you a quote in two or three hours—sound good?" nearly every single person says, "Okay."

Even if someone is ready to buy, if you're the one saying they can't get a quote until later, you've removed the opportunity to close right then. They're saying "okay" because they have no other choice. So let's make it a habit: get comfortable closing in person. Now you may be thinking, *What if I don't know everything involved in the project and I need time to price the job?* That is actually a process problem. The closing rate goes down so dramatically when you leave the property that you must take time to learn how to quickly assess the costs of the job. Take some time to invest in a system that allows you to accurately price jobs on the spot. In most cases, you're quoting the same types of jobs repeatedly, and you already know the common pitfalls. Even if you don't, it's still worth it to close the deal, even if you need to add a small incidental cost.

Consistency

This is something I often stress to my team. In sales, you need a consistent sales process. That means doing things the same way every single time.

Why? Because you need to know what's working—and what's not. If you're constantly changing your approach, how will you ever pinpoint what's effective?

Here's an example:

Let's say you go on ten sales calls and don't close a single one. But if you followed the same sales process each time, at least now you know that specific process isn't working, and you can adjust accordingly. Without consistency, you're just guessing.

So you change the process. You run it on another ten sales calls, and this time you close three out of ten.

Great! Now tweak one element and try again. Maybe your close rate will go up or down, but either way, you're learning. You cannot test and improve if you're doing things differently every time. That kind of consistency is the foundation for tracking, evaluating, and ultimately improving your sales success.

Believe it or not—and if you own a business, especially a trades business, you'll relate to this—most of the time, we don't have a sales process at all. I can't tell you how many times I've asked my clients to describe their sales process, and almost all of them say, "Well, I don't really have one."

Okay. That's not a good sign. At the bare minimum, you need a sales process—even if it's a bad one—because if you're consistent, you can test it, tweak it, and change your results.

Remember: Sales is a relationship. The more you give, the more likely you are to close.

And giving is simply serving. You ask question after question after question until the client tells you where the pain is. Then, you offer the exact "medicine" they need.

They are far more likely to buy because your offer is tailored exactly to what they want.

Framework for Closing Sales: Step-by-Step

1. Build rapport throughout the sales process. Don't just talk business—be human. Be a trusted advisor. Be someone in the community who's there to help them make a good decision.

2. Ask questions to discover their true wants and needs.

3. Use their answers to tailor your recommendations.

4. Listen carefully and base your offer on what they've shared.

5. Make the offer that best matches their needs.

6. Don't give people what they don't want or need. That's not serving—it's selling blindly.

7. Ask for the sale. Go ahead and ask: "Can I ring you up?" In the trades, we say: "Would you like me to schedule the job for today?" Ask directly. Ask confidently.

Common Mistakes and Quick Fixes

Here's a big mistake: not following up. You've heard me say it before—you have to ask for the sale right then and there. But what happens when someone says no? They'll throw out some kind of objection. We'll get into objections later, but for now, let's say you didn't close the deal on the spot. What do you do? Here's a simple fix: follow up with them later.

Most sales happen after the first conversation. One of the biggest mistakes people make is assuming that following up is annoying. I've had plenty of clients say, "I don't want to keep calling—they'll get irritated." No, they won't. They asked you for a quote, which means they need something you offer.

Following up is simply you being a good person, checking in and asking if they have any other questions. So, get that head trash out. (Yes, we've talked about head trash before.) Get it out of your head and put it in the trash—the idea that following up is annoying. The only time following up is annoying is when someone says, "Do not contact me again," and you contact them anyway. Don't do that. But otherwise, it's perfectly okay to follow up—especially if you set that expectation ahead of time.

One thing I always do: if I don't close the deal right at the table, I make it clear that I'll be following up. I'll say something like, "Hey, it's my job to follow up with you. When's a good day for me to do that?" Typically, they'll tell you the best time for them, and that's gold. When someone says, "You can call me tomorrow after I get off work," they've just told you exactly when to reach out.

Now, when you call, it's not annoying—they remember they asked you to call at five o'clock. See? So toss that head trash that says following up is a bad thing.

Following up actually changes the game. It sets you apart from probably 90% of companies, because most of them don't bother to follow up. Remember, they invited you in.

The Lake vs. the Ocean: An Analogy from Ariel Robinson

Ariel Robinson once taught me this analogy: You want to be like a lake, not like an ocean.

Now think about it. When you stand at the edge of the ocean, you hear the waves crashing. The ocean is violent. It's aggressive. It's chaotic. But when you stand by a lake, it's peaceful. The water is still. You hear birds chirping, animals in the distance—it's calm.

You need to keep your mind like that lake: calm, neutral, and not emotionally reactive. When you carry all these preconceived notions— like "sales is sleazy" or "follow-ups are annoying"—your thoughts become like the ocean. Everything is crashing around inside your head.

So be the lake. Be neutral. Don't let your assumptions interfere with the sales process. Stay calm. Stay consistent.

Emotional Intelligence in Sales

Now remember: Being imperfect is being human. Lean into that— don't try to hide from it. When I was selling in my early years, I wanted to be perfect, especially when I was inside a customer's home. I tried to be an extreme professional. Everything I said had to be flawless. I couldn't make a mistake.

And if I tripped in someone's yard or nearly fell, I'd feel embarrassed, like I'd ruined the entire deal. But here's the truth: When you make a mistake in front of a customer—when your computer freezes, something malfunctions, or things go sideways—you become more human.

It reminds them of themselves. It reminds them of their own job and the mistakes they make.

And now, instead of being a cold sales robot who sounds like dollar signs, you're just a real person doing your best. So lean into imperfection. It helps you connect.

You always want to read the room—it's called "mirroring." I always tell my sales team: "You don't want to be a comedian to customers who don't like to laugh." What I mean by that is this: if you're in someone's home giving an estimate, and the customer is very serious—stern, all business—don't be the joker. Be serious. But always be yourself. It's totally fine to crack a joke now and then, but don't turn into a clown. Now, on the flip side—if your customer is super friendly, they open the door with a big smile, they're making jokes, tapping you on the shoulder, asking about your kids—don't be the cold, serious guy.

If they're nodding, you nod.

If they're joking, you joke. Simple.

You don't have to become them, but you do need to read the room. I always say: "Laugh with those who laugh. Be serious with those who are serious."

Sales wins in transformations. For many years, early in my career, I was too professional and clinical because I thought that's what people wanted—the "super professional" salesperson. But my closing rate didn't really take off until I became more human. Less stiff. More relaxed. I started making personal connections—talking about my family, where I'm from, and finding common ground with the customer. That rapport-based approach made a huge difference. In fact, my closing rate increased by 20% when I embraced imperfection and focused on building human connections. When you learn how to build rapport and master timing, your closing rate will jump.

That's why I always teach people how to be human in sales, because it usually makes all the difference.

Conclusion: Stop Pitching, Start Serving.

Don't focus on pushing or pitching offers. Focus on understanding the customer's problem and offering the solution that best addresses it.

Remember: ask better questions—and ask more than one. Try to go four or five questions deep. When you build stronger connections, your closing rate will absolutely go up.

Selling isn't talking. Selling is listening, serving, and offering the next right step tailored to your client. That's the core of it.

What I like to do, because every industry is different, is write down at least eight questions that focus on the common objections a business owner typically has. For example, I may walk into someone's home or office, and the first thing I want to know—question number one—is very basic: "What brings me here today?" or "What can I help you with?" That's always my starting point.

The rest of the questions are usually designed to uncover potential objections. For instance, some businesses might ask: "What's your budget?" This is because pricing is often an objection, and it helps you quickly determine whether the customer is budget-conscious.

One person might say, "Well, I don't really care about the budget. I want the best unit on the market." *Boom!* You already know where to guide that conversation.

Another customer might say, "I don't have much of a budget. I've been trying to save up." Now you know you should offer something more budget-friendly.

So those common objections, like price, are key. You want to ask questions that tap into what's on the customer's mind. That way, you can tailor your offer directly to their needs. And remember, this varies from industry to industry.

Now, here's what I typically do. I've helped a lot of companies with their sales processes, and I always say: "If you have no sales process at all, start with the fundamentals."

From there, we can focus on improving it over time. The first step when building a sales process is to ensure you're building rapport throughout the entire conversation. The reason I emphasize that is because people often only build rapport at the beginning, during the greeting, and again at the end when they're about to leave.

But it's important to find moments throughout the conversation to connect. Look for shared experiences, common interests, anything that builds trust. Next, if you don't already have multiple options to offer, create them. For example, if you only sell one widget, or you run a lawn care business and only offer basic front and back yard cutting, you need to expand. Add services like tree trimming, edging, or even custom service packages. So before your next sales call, make sure you have a menu of options ready. That's your second foundational step.

Then, establish your follow-up process, even if it's basic. You might decide to follow up two days later, then four days after that, and again six days after that. Just choose a schedule and stick to it. Once that's in place, you can begin to refine and enhance it over time. Once you've tightened up your sales game and you're converting leads with confidence, it's time to turn on the faucet. Marketing is how you keep the phones ringing. But not all marketing is created equal. In the next chapter, we'll break down the difference between wasted ad spend and real lead flow, and show you how to invest in marketing that actually moves the needle for your business.

CHAPTER 6

The Gold Mine You Forgot— Your Customer List

One of the fastest ways to increase revenue in your business is to go straight to the customers who have already bought from you. Your customer list is the undefeated, unmatched asset in your business. It's your most powerful—and most overlooked—resource.

Time and time again, businesses tend to look at advertising as the solution. When things get slow, the first question is often, "What do I need to do to bring in new customers?" But in reality, you've already brought in lots of customers.

You don't necessarily need new ones—you just need your existing customers to come back. Sure, there's always a place for marketing and advertising. But if you need money now, if you need sales and revenue immediately, your customer list will convert much faster than someone who's never heard of you.

In truth, the people who've bought from you before, you've already paid for them. Think about it: You've run ads, attended community events, handed out flyers, and posted on social media. People saw those efforts, came in, and bought from you. That means you already invested in acquiring them. So why pay to acquire new customers if you need fast cash?

Go back to the customers you've already paid to reach. Don't waste that investment.

Existing customers already trust you. They've vetted you. They've seen your ads, your trucks on the road, your business signs, they've looked you up, read your reviews, and decided: "I like this business. I'm going to buy from them." So you don't have to build that trust again.

They've also demonstrated proven purchase behavior. They bought once—they're more likely to buy again. If you sell shirts, they're probably wearing one. If you do lawn care and cut their grass all last year, and now it's the off-season, they're more likely to use you again.

So instead of printing more flyers to try and attract new customers, why not reach out to the ones you already served? For example, "Hey, I cut your grass all last year. It's starting to grow again—let's get you back on the schedule before your lawn becomes the worst on the block." That kind of outreach results in a much higher closing rate than cold marketing to strangers. And the best part? You already have their contact information.

Whether you're using a CRM or even just pen and paper like it's 1999, you have their info. All you have to do is reach out.

One of my go-to messages, and we'll talk more about messaging later in this book, is: *"Hey, this is Michael from [XYZ] Heating and Cooling. I worked on your system six months ago—now it's time for a service."*

That phrase "I worked on your system" is powerful. That's a personal connection. Remember when we talked about building rapport? This is the ultimate form of it—they already know you, and you have their history.

When I consult for a business, there are two main strategies I use to increase revenue very quickly.

Number one: Raise your prices.

Number two: Reach out to your existing customers. And there's a reason for that.

Think about this scenario: It's a Saturday afternoon, and your spouse wants to go on a date. It's time for some quality husband-and-wife time. My wife often says, "Hey, let's go get something to eat." But most of the time, she doesn't know what she wants to eat. Now, does it make sense for me to start suggesting places she's never been to before? Probably not. That would turn into a long and drawn-out conversation. There's a much better chance she'll choose a place if I name somewhere she's already been and liked. So I say, "Why not try this place?" Why? Because she's already vetted it. She trusts it.

Now, think about this in terms of business. Why aren't we going back to the customers who have already bought from us? Customers who've purchased from you once are much more likely to buy from you again. So go straight to them. In fact, someone recently asked me,

"What was the biggest thing that changed your business? What brought in the most revenue?" And the answer—without a doubt—was reaching out to my customer list consistently.

So, how do you generate quick wins with past customers? There are a few strategies you need to follow because your customer list is a gold mine. It's your most important asset, next to your employees.

But you can't just reach out haphazardly and risk damaging those relationships. So let's go over a couple of effective strategies.

Email

You really need to be emailing your customers. Email isn't going anywhere. Despite all the recent changes in technology—especially with artificial intelligence—email has been around for a long time, and it's deeply entrenched in our daily lives. But too many businesses aren't emailing their customers. Now, retail businesses have this nailed down.

You can't go to a store like Target without them asking for your email. And if you give it to them, you'll get emails constantly—probably more than twice a month. Some businesses email every other day.

One of my clients runs a large retail chain, and she emails her customer list every other day. That's a lot. Yet she says her unsubscribe rate is very low. Why? Because she's not emailing strangers—she's emailing people who already like her product.

You need to do the same. You already have their email. Remind them who you are.

And let's be honest—we forget the businesses we've used. For example, when you had your roof replaced, do you remember the name of the company that did it? Or when you had your grass cut last year—do you remember who did it? Chances are, you don't. And as a business owner, that's a scary place to be.

It sends chills down my spine to think I might have customers who've used me multiple times, but they can't remember my business name. What does that mean? It means that when they need me again in six months, they're going to go to Google and search *"heating and air conditioning company near me."* And guess what? All of my competitors are going to show up.

I don't want that. So, I email my customers and make sure I'm in their inbox at least a couple of times per month. That way, when they need me, they've seen my name enough times that they don't google *"heating and cooling company near me."* Instead, they google my company name, or better yet, they go straight to their inbox, reply to my email, and contact me directly.

And just like that, my competitors are completely out of the conversation. You have to get used to emailing.

And the beautiful thing about email is that you can reuse emails. That's one of my big secrets. I have around 20 emails. I send an email twice per month, which gives me just under a year's worth of content. And I recycle those emails. I used the same email at the beginning of June when it hit 100 degrees here. I copy and paste it year after year after year. And you know what? I've never had a customer in twenty years reply and say, "Hey, I caught you! You used the same email twice." Nobody cares about that. The point is to have consistent touchpoints.

Text Messaging

Text messaging is an even more powerful tool, but you have to be cautious. It's more invasive than email, and if you overdo it or make it too transactional, you'll get blocked quickly—we'll talk about that in a second. But for industries like heating and cooling, plumbing, or lawn care, you absolutely should be texting.

At a minimum, I recommend texting every six months. But you can even stretch that to once per month, depending on your approach.

Keep in mind: text messaging is more invasive than email, so the more often you do it, the higher the chance someone will block you. So, if you're going to text your customers, make sure it's worth it—not to you, but to them.

Remember: selling is serving. So, don't send a text that's all about you. Make sure it provides value to them, because they're the ones who decide whether to block you or not.

You can automate all of this with technology. You'll get sick. You'll take vacations. You'll take days off. But technology doesn't sleep—and it doesn't forget.

In my business, I wrote a full set of text messages once—three years' worth. Now, every customer receives a text message every six months for the next three years. It all happens automatically, like clockwork, because the software handles it.

And it's an incredible way to stay top of mind. This is how you become "that person's company." You know when someone says, "I've got a really good guy who cuts my lawn, you should use him," and the other person replies, "Oh, I've already got a guy." That's the position you want to be in. You become someone's guy or someone's gal by staying top of mind, so that when they need you, they can find you.

One thing that really scares me as a business owner is when I hear someone say, "I used to have a company I really loved. I used them all the time, but I just can't remember the name anymore. So I can't find them." That terrifies me. Because if I'm not reaching out and reminding people who I am, they're having that same conversation about my company.

And we'll dive deeper into that in the branding section of this book. But remember: people forget business names—even when they love your service. I mean, you probably don't even remember what you had for breakfast this morning.

And unfortunately, you've probably forgotten the names of many of your friends' kids. I'll admit it—I'm ashamed to say that when I visit friends with very young children, I often forget their kids' names. It's not because I don't care; we're just forgetful as human beings. So if you can't recall your breakfast, chances are you don't remember the name of the auto mechanic who fixed your car last year.

That's not great for them. The takeaway? You need to stay top of mind with your customers.

Consistent outreach keeps you front and center when they need you again. Here's a business tip (maybe even a secret): most companies only reach out to their customers when they're desperate for sales. And that's a big mistake.

Don't make it a habit to reach out only when times are tough. If you connect with your audience consistently and genuinely, you'll never have to write a desperate message again.

Warm Leads vs. Cold Leads

Warm leads convert faster and more easily. But let's be honest—many businesses avoid messaging their customers because of emotional fears and "head trash." For example: "I don't want to be annoying." I can't tell you how many times I've encouraged business owners to send a text or an email to their customers, only to hear that same tired excuse: "I don't want to annoy them."

But mindset is everything.

Nobody's day is ruined because they got an email from their lawn care provider reminding them it's time to apply weed treatment. In fact, most people would welcome that kind of message.

As someone who owns a heating company, I send out messages in the fall that say, "Winter storms are coming—make sure you do [XYZ] so your pipes don't freeze." People love that kind of helpful nudge.

That's not annoying. What is annoying is messaging only when you want something. But when you send helpful, value-driven content, whether via email or text, you're providing a service and keeping your business top of mind.

Shift the mindset. Remember, this isn't cold calling—we're talking about communicating with your existing customers. These people invited you into their lives. They gave you their contact information. Use it responsibly. Use it wisely.

Provide value, not just promotions. This is where many businesses go wrong. We get selfish. We think every message should be, "Buy this!" or "Come in now!" Don't do that.

The goal of reaching out to your customer list is to provide ongoing value throughout the year. That way, when you do hit a slow month and need to boost revenue, you've earned the right to ask. Think about it: who enjoys a one-sided relationship where someone only reaches out when they need something? No one. But what about the friend who's always helping you—giving you advice, picking you up from the airport, even loaning you money? When that friend asks for help, you jump at the chance.

Be that kind of business.

We need to emulate that same approach in business. You need to give, give, give before you ask, ask, ask. Telemarketers are annoying for a simple reason: they only call you when they want to sell you something. They're just strangers. They call you for the first time and say, "Hey, we've got this thing—come buy it." You're not going to be that person. You're going to provide value first, and then you're going to make an offer.

Use Segmentation

In my business, I have thousands of customers because I've been doing this for over twenty years. Whether you have thousands of customers or just a hundred, you don't want to send the same exact message to your entire customer list.

Think about it: If you're a plumber and you've already installed a new toilet at a customer's house, you don't want to send them a message offering a discount on new toilets. That's not helpful to them. You want to segment your list based on who bought what, and who needs what.

You're going to group all the people who have already bought a certain product into one list and name that list. Then you'll create another list for those who bought something else, so you know who's who and which message to send to whom. Remember when we talked about how selling is about offering what people need? Your message is going to fall flat if your customer list isn't segmented.

My own customer list is broken into several groups. I have a list of people who bought an air conditioning system in the last year. I have another list of people who bought air conditioning five years ago. I have a list of people with systems that are ten years old. I also have separate lists for realtors, property managers, and landlords. That way, when I send an email, it makes sense to the person receiving it. Because if the message isn't relevant, people will start unsubscribing from your emails. They'll start blocking your text messages. And when you're blocked by email or text, that's a lot of lost revenue, because your customer list represents the people who are most likely to buy from you.

If you can't reach them because you kept asking and weren't being a good "friend"—always taking, never giving—you're hurting your business. So segment your list. For example, if you have a list of realtors, you can send them tips for pre-sale home inspections. If you have a list of property managers, send them emails or texts with tips to reduce maintenance issues.

If someone just bought a new heating and cooling system, send them tips on how to extend the system's life. Make sure every message is relevant to the recipient. If you haven't already, take some time to go through your customer list and segment it.

Hopefully, you're using some kind of email or text message software so that you're not manually sending each message. It would be a nightmare for me to send 10,000 emails one by one. I write one email, send it to 10,000 people—done.

Messaging Frequency

You should be reaching out at least once or twice per month. You have to keep your business top of mind.

You don't want to wait too long, because you never know when someone will need your service. One to two times per month is a good baseline.

That said, every business is different. When I talk about *results*, you need to test and adjust. If you're sending one to two times per month and no one is complaining, you might be able to ramp it up to four times per month.

On the other hand, if you're getting a lot of unsubscribes, you might need to cut back—or check your messaging to make sure you're not being too self-focused. Also, avoid one-size-fits-all messages. That's where segmentation comes in.

Real Story: When the List Saved the Business

I had a client who was panicking during the slow winter season. They came to me saying, "Michael, we're trying everything. We're advertising. We're going to community events. But nobody's calling us. It's been weeks, and we're running out of money."

I said, "Why don't we text your customers?"

Their first reaction was the usual: "Well... I don't want to be annoying."

So I asked, "Do we need money or not?"

They agreed.

They had 1,500 customers on their list. We wrote a personal, thoughtful message, and they filled their schedule.

It wasn't a surprise to me. You're reaching out to people who have already bought from you. Your customer list is your gold mine.

Do you remember those old commercials that used to come on in the middle of the night?

Hopefully, you're old enough to remember them—or maybe I'm just dating myself. They always ended with something like, "While supplies last!" That's urgency. For example, say: "We're running this deal until Friday." People are more likely to act when they feel a time limit.

And then you need a call to action. What do you want them to do after they read the message? I always like to end with an open-ended question in every text message. Something like, *"Can I schedule this for you?"* When you ask a question, people feel compelled to respond—it's common courtesy.

They'll likely say yes or no. And even if they say no, that's okay. You've started a conversation.

You can follow up with something like: *"Okay, when would be a better time for me to schedule it for you?"*

So, remember: a strong call to action matters. I talk more about this in the "Messaging" section of this book.

The result for the client I mentioned earlier? Thousands of dollars in booked work in one day.

Before that, they had spent weeks and weeks marketing with zero results. But when they followed this approach—*Boom!* Bookings flooded in. It works. It always works.

The Long-Term Value of List Building

Don't just focus on selling. Your goal isn't just to go out, get customers, do the work, and get paid. You should also be building your customer list year-round. If you don't already have something in your workflow that adds customers to your list, make it a priority. Here's how:

Let's say you're branding your company. You should be doing community events—showing up and being visible. Have one of your wrapped trucks there (if you're in the home service business), and make sure you set up a branded table with your logo and materials.

But don't stop there. Make sure you're collecting names, phone numbers, and emails. Every single marketing activity should include a way to capture contact information.

This is how your list grows. Every year, your customer list should be getting bigger and bigger. That way, when you need business, you already have people to reach out to.

Imagine your customer list as a bucket full of people. You always want to keep that bucket full—because people move, things change. So keep adding to your bucket. Why? Because customers move away. Their buying habits change. You're losing people all the time—it's just a fact of doing business. So, you need to keep refilling the bucket. Always be adding to your list. Some people won't buy now, but they'll buy later. And if they're on your list and you're consistently reminding them who you are, you'll be in a great position to close the sale when the time is right.

If they're already on your list and you're consistently reminding them who you are, you're in a strong position to close the sale. When you're advertising, make sure to use forms and offer incentives to collect information. For example: "Get 10% off when you fill out this form." Then, follow up with targeted campaigns.

Of course, there are a few important things you should never do:

Do not blast irrelevant messages to your entire list: Always segment your list and send relevant content to the right audience.

Don't neglect your customers once the job is done: Nobody likes to feel abandoned. Think about it—have you ever bought something from a company, and then they just disappeared? If someone buys from you—even if they've already purchased everything you offer—continue to nurture that relationship. Share helpful content like:

- Tips and tricks
- Educational emails
- Useful advice for maintaining their home, car, or other services

This keeps you top of mind. So when they need you again—or know someone else who does—they remember how much you helped and are more likely to refer others to you.

Your list is your lifeline. Your past customers are your fastest path to new revenue. Make sure you automate your outreach, personalize it by segmenting your list, and use clear, valuable messaging. Most importantly, systematize your communication. Don't just panic and blast out desperate messages asking people to buy from you when revenue is low. Instead, plan your outreach thoughtfully and spread it throughout the year. A well-segmented customer list is not only a survival tool—it's a growth engine.

I can speak to this from years of customer experience. One of the biggest reasons businesses neglect their customer list is that they misunderstand how real people operate in their day-to-day lives. For example, if you're a lawn care company, you might think, *They called me last time their grass got long, so they'll call me again.*

But that's not how it works. People forget. We're all busy. Moms are driving one kid to soccer practice, another to rehearsal, juggling work, managing the household, and squeezing in a date night. There's just too much going on. You're not top of mind.

So what happens? When they do need your service, they just google someone, and they may pick the first name that shows up. We have to solve that forgetfulness.

A Simple Fix: Be Proactive

Here's an example from my own life: I like my lawn to be cut regularly. I hate when it gets long and messy. But I'm busy, and every time I think to call the lawn care guy, something else comes up. I still want the service—I'm just too busy to initiate it. But imagine if my lawn care provider called me and said, "Hey Mike, it's been two weeks. I'm sure your grass is long—want me to come by?"

I'd say, "Yes! Please do. I've been meaning to call you."

See, most people are ready—they just need a reminder.

Business owners often assume customers will call when they're ready, but that's giving people too much credit. It's on us to take the responsibility and say: "Hey, it's time for your oil change. I haven't seen you in three months."

Most customers will reply, "Oh man, yeah, thanks for reminding me."

When you shift your mindset from waiting for the customer to serving the customer, your business becomes much more successful.

This is something I actually do in my coaching program, though I don't have an official name for it yet.

I believe every company should show up as a member of the community. Here's what I mean:

We all show up as individuals. You might see Michael Johnson at church, Walmart, or the local festival. As a person, I'm part of the community. But rarely do people see your business as a "person" in the community. That's where community events come into play.

If your town has a big annual festival, your business should show up there too—not just you personally. You should have a booth, branded signage, and engage as a business.

If there's a local nonprofit, like a food bank, you might volunteer personally. That's great. But ask yourself: *When does my business show up as a member of the community?*

When you volunteer, wear your company shirt. Wear your branded hat. Let it be clear that it's not just you volunteering—your business is there. Your business is:

- Donating to the food bank
- Sponsoring the local initiative
- Showing up at the Dogwood Festival, handing out waters

Wherever members of the community go, your business needs to go, too. Generating leads is one thing—attracting the *right* customers is another. You don't want to be the cheapest guy in town, running around for people who don't value what you do. In this next chapter, we'll talk about how to stop chasing price shoppers and start drawing in homeowners who respect your time, trust your expertise, and say yes without hesitation.

CHAPTER 7

Branding with Teeth—Crafting an Identity That Cuts Through the Noise

What does it really mean to have a brand with teeth?

A strong brand stands out—even when customers aren't actively shopping. But what does that actually mean? It's incredibly important, and I'll explain why.

Let me give you an analogy. I'm not a car person. I couldn't care less about cars—seriously. When I'm driving around, stuck in traffic, I usually don't pay attention to the types of cars on the road. I don't care. But every once in a blue moon, a car drives by in a ridiculously loud color, like bright orange or fire-engine red. And I'll glance over to my wife and say, "That's a pretty color. Look at that car over there."

She'll look and say, "That is nice. It's different." Now remember, neither of us cares about cars. But that car stood out. It was so different that we noticed. And that's the essence of branding.

Too often, businesses blend in because they're not even trying to stand out. Dan Antonelli, the author of *Branded Not Blanded*, is a master of this idea. He emphasizes how so many brands today are just bland.

They're boring. They're forgettable.

Think of your business like a car on the road. There are people—like me—who couldn't care less about cars. So what are you going to do to make those people notice you? Because let's face it: brand invisibility is real—until the customer enters the buying phase.

Take me, again. I don't care about cars. But every couple of years, I need a new one. When that time comes, the process starts from scratch. I don't know much about cars, so I just drive to the dealership and look at the inventory. But by that point, it's too late for a brand to make an impression. I need a car in a couple of days. I don't have time to develop a connection with a brand. So I pick whatever's available. But what if a brand had made an impression six months before my car broke down? Then, when I walk into the dealership, I'd say, "Hey, do you have any of [that brand] in stock?" And just like that, they make a sale.

That's what branding is. It's about making an impression before the customer starts shopping. That's the core of it.

We don't want brand invisibility. We want our brand to create a visual—and more importantly, emotional—impact. We want to build a brand so memorable that it becomes the customer's default choice before they even think about buying.

Let me give you another example. I have a friend who owns a plumbing business about an hour from here. I've known him for years. I don't serve his area, but I have friends who live there. When they ask me for a plumber, I say, "Use my friend!" And I give his name, but I never remembered the name of his business. And he's my friend.

Why? Because his brand was boring. It didn't stick. But recently, he rebranded and added a story behind the brand.

He's a huge dog lover, so he partnered with a local dog shelter and now donates a percentage of his profits to them. He even changed his business name to reflect this passion. He called it Plumbing Hounds. And now? I'll never forget it because it's tied to a story. It's tied to something he cares about. Something I care about. And the name reflects that emotional connection.

So I went from saying, "Oh yeah, I have a friend in that town. Let me find his name and number, and then I'll send it to you," to simply saying, "Hey, go use Plumbing Hounds." Why? Because it was tied to an emotion.

The Bible and Homer's *The Iliad* are examples of stories that have endured for generations. Let's talk about the Bible for a minute. Religious or not, it's undeniable that the Bible is the most-read and most-sold book in human history. Second to that is Homer's *The Iliad*. What these two books have in common is storytelling. The Bible is full of stories—it's not a textbook. It's a collection of narratives: This person did this, and here's how it affected their life. That person did that, and here's the outcome.

The Iliad? One insanely long, epic story.

If you can use stories, you can touch people's hearts. When you tie a story into your brand, your company becomes far more memorable. That's why major corporations invest heavily in commercials that tell stories. Sometimes it's funny, sometimes it's emotional, but they're always aiming to connect.

You'll see these big brands partnering with causes and crafting campaigns that tell a narrative. Now, if Starbucks can become the second biggest restaurant chain in the world—not by selling food, but by selling an experience—then you can absolutely become the biggest plumbing company in your town. We don't have to be Disney. We don't have to be the most-sold product on the planet. But we can be the most well-known name in our community by using stories.

That's the secret. Too often, we focus on telling people what we do: "I fix air conditioners. I install air conditioners. I do maintenance on air conditioners." Let's be honest—that's boring.

How about this instead? "I'm the son of a tradesman. My dad was a mechanic. His dad was a mechanic. And his dad before him was a mechanic. I grew up on the shelves of a hardware store. So it was only natural for me to go into a business where I fix things. That's why I started my HVAC company."

Which version is more memorable? Of course, it's the story. Because brands that connect through stories sell more, stick longer, and build deeper loyalty.

What Makes a Brand Irresistible?

When a brand tells a personal, specific, and relatable story, it becomes irresistible. I call this having an "irresistible identity." It's something that connects your customer to something they care about. Because remember—nobody cares about your business. People only hire you because they need something.

Unless it's your mom. Your mom buys from you because she loves you. But let's face it—you can't build a business just off your mom. So you need to connect your brand to something other people care about.

I even do an exercise to test this. I say, "Okay, let's see if your brand really has an irresistible identity or not." I often tell people: "Write a paragraph about your business. Once you've written that paragraph, take an eraser and remove everything in it that your competitors could also say. What are you left with?"

Let me explain what I mean with an example. Say I run an air conditioning business. I fix and install air conditioners. I have lots of five-star reviews. I'm passionate about my work. I believe we're the best at what we do.

Okay—but how many other businesses can say the exact same thing? A lot.

Plenty of businesses have five-star reviews—erase that. Many fix air conditioners—erase that. Most are passionate about what they do— erase that, too.

Now, let's replace those with things no one else can claim. For example, I started my air conditioning business twenty years ago after leaving the military. We're a veteran-owned company. I'm the son of a tradesman, who was also the son of a tradesman. I have twenty years of experience layered on top of a childhood spent working alongside my father, doing this very trade.

Now, if I try to erase parts that my competitors could say, I'm not erasing anything—because that story is personal. That story is unique.

It's sticky. It resonates. People connect with "veteran-owned." They connect with the image of a young boy learning a trade from his father. That's an irresistible identity.

Customers are drawn to that kind of authenticity. But if your website just says, *"I fix plumbing. I'm good at it. I have five-star reviews,"* that's not irresistible—that's forgettable.

Your brand story should connect with your local community or your customers' values. It has to go beyond visuals. Too often, we think branding starts with a logo and picking a color palette. That's fine— visuals help. They get attention. Like when I'm driving and I see a car with a striking color, and I say, "Wow, that's pretty." That gets me to notice.

But what gets someone to buy once they've noticed? It's the things other businesses can't offer. It's the story, the values, the meaning.

So ask yourself: *What are my values? Who am I? Who owns the business? Why did they start it? What's the tone and personality of my brand? And what kind of impact does my business have?*

If you donate part of your profits to the local dog shelter—that's impact. If you and your team volunteer at the food bank on weekends—that's impact. These are the stories people remember. These are the stories people buy into.

It's not just about what you do. "I'm a mechanic. I'm a lawn care person." Sure—but your values, your tone, your impact, and your relatable story are what make your brand irresistible.

That's how you become the person customers stick with, even when competitors come knocking. When someone tries to undercut you and knocks on your customer's door, they say, "No thanks, I already got a guy." And it's not because of what you do—it's because of everything else we're talking about here.

It happened to me.

I remember being at a customer's house. She had been with me for ten years. I was doing some work, and there was a local competitor who used to drive around town. When he saw an air conditioning van, he'd park up the street and wait for the van to leave. Then he'd knock on the door and say, "Hey, I saw this company at your place, but I can offer the same thing."

And he did that to me. As soon as I left, he knocked on her door and said, "Hey, I can do this—and cheaper."

And you know what she did? She handed his flyer back and said, "No thanks, I'm not interested." Why would she stay with me if she could get it cheaper?

Because of my values.

Because of my impact.

Because of my identity.

My entire brand—and the story behind it—made an impact on her.

Irresistible brands evoke emotion and raise perceived value.

The Brand-Building Process

So, take some time today—after reading this chapter—to do the following exercise.

Write a paragraph about your business. Then, take out your eraser and delete every single phrase that could apply to your competitors in your town. For example: fast service? Lots of businesses claim that. Five-star reviews? Plenty of people have those too. Now, look at what's left.

Do you have anything unique remaining? If not, you don't yet have a customer story. And that's okay. This is where you start. Focus on what's uniquely true for you—the things no one else can say.

When you do that, you'll be very, very hard to compete with—because you know this, and your competitors don't. Why? Because you're reading this book, and they're not. So start identifying those key elements.

Some people say, "But I don't have a unique story." I've heard that from clients before. But the truth is that everyone has a unique story. We are all unique by design. God created each of us with a purpose. He forged your path.

So start identifying your differences. Ask yourself: *Is my business veteran-owned? Do I support a cause? Do I have a generational legacy? Has my family been in this business for years? Did my father pass the business down to me? Or did no one pass anything down—did I just see a need and decide to fulfill it?*

Everyone has a story. Your brand needs to reflect yours.

So take time for some inward reflection. Ask yourself why you started this business. I guarantee the reason is tied to something others can relate to.

Voice, Tone, and Positioning

Your voice should reflect your company's character and your customers' lifestyle. Because here's the truth: Your customers don't care that you started a business.

Your mom cares. But they don't. So, what does your customer care about? And how can you connect your story to what they care about?

It's no coincidence that in my business, I've emphasized being veteran-owned, because my business is in a town that has the largest military base in the United States. Our town is full of veterans, so being veteran-owned aligns with my customers' lifestyle. It's something they can connect with—values that tie you and your customers together and give you an irresistible identity. Storytelling builds trust and emotional connection.

And remember, a great brand should always make people feel safe and seen. It should make them feel proud, and it should make them feel aligned or connected to you.

If your brand is making people feel the opposite, erase that paragraph and start over. If your brand doesn't make people feel safe—because remember, it's not about you, it's about them—then it's time to reflect and create your customer story.

How Branding Fuels Sales and Marketing

Branding is not just marketing fluff—it directly impacts conversions. Now, imagine my company is veteran-owned. A veteran sees that, reads it, and immediately feels a connection. They know I understand them. Remember the sales process we talked about in Chapter 4? Well, I've already built rapport before I even meet them, because my brand has made a personal connection.

So, the rapport starts before I even meet the person. Do you see how branding connects with sales—and ultimately drives revenue? A strong brand removes doubt. A weak brand dilutes even the best offer. Because if you have no brand, no story, no customer connection, no irresistible identity—you're just a price. And you'd better be the cheapest price, because that's all you have to offer.

Trust = Frequency + Consistency + Proof

Here are a couple of things you can do to make your brand stronger and increase trust:

Use Team Photos

Nobody wants a faceless business, especially in the home service industry. When we invite someone into our home, whether it's to fix plumbing, cut the grass, or repair an air conditioning system, we want to know who's coming.

I want to see who's coming into my home before they arrive. Team photos increase trust.

If your website shows real people, customers can look and think, *Oh, they seem friendly.* That alone puts you a step ahead of faceless companies. Otherwise, customers are left thinking, *I won't know if this person is safe until they ring the doorbell.* That does not build trust.

Share Awards and Reviews

If you've been in business for any amount of time, you've probably earned some kind of award, even if it's small. Joined the Chamber of Commerce? That's a trust signal. Won a "Best of the Town" award—even from a tiny local newspaper? Who cares? You won it. You own it. Put that on your website.

For example: "Voted Best of [Town] by [Newspaper Name]."

Showcase Real Reviews

Don't just say, "I have 800 reviews."

Copy and paste them onto your website. Include the customer's name. Remember, they posted those reviews online with their names already. So forget the head trash that tells you, *I don't want to post this; they might not be okay with it.* They already posted it. It's public.

Tell Your Origin Story Often

Your origin story is one of the most powerful tools you have to build a real emotional connection with your audience. In my business, every brochure, every flyer, every website, and almost every single video ad talks about our story. Very rarely will you interact with my business and not know that we're a veteran-owned business. So, you don't want to go through the process of crafting your brand story, building your branding, and then letting it sit in a drawer somewhere, forgotten.

Your brand story is meant to be forward-facing. Even your logo should reflect that story in some way. Here's an analogy for you: A stranger in the woods becomes more trustworthy if they're walking with someone. So, let me paint this picture for you. Step into this world just for a moment. You're walking alone in the woods, taking a quiet stroll because you need time to reflect. Off in the distance, you notice a man walking toward you. A little scary, isn't it? Now, what if that man is walking with his wife? Still a little uncertain—you don't know either of them—but slightly less scary. There's more than one person.

Let's ramp it up further. What if that couple is pushing a stroller with a baby in it? Now you're starting to feel a bit safer. What if that same couple is walking with a tour guide, and the guide is pointing out sights and facts along the trail? Now it's really not that scary. And finally, what if there's also a police officer nearby? At this point, you're not scared at all. You're looking at a family on a guided nature tour with a police presence—not strangers in the woods.

Your business is often like a stranger in the woods. People don't know who to trust. They're trying to hire someone, and a company shows up saying, "I'm trustworthy." But that's not enough.

You stop being a stranger when:

- You add trust badges to your website.
- You're a member of the Chamber of Commerce.
- You volunteer with the local police or give back to the community.
- You start bringing other people into your brand story.

Now you're a family-owned company that supports the police department, helps out at the local food bank, and is known in the community.

Never let your business be "just a stranger." Put faces to it. Add awards to it. Include your community in it. It's a lot less intimidating than a random person by themselves saying, "I can come to your house and sell you something."

Case Study: A Rebrand That Worked

I'll be honest—my business used to be forgettable. For the first ten years, I heard the same painful feedback over and over again. I'd show up at a customer's house to fix their air conditioning system, and they'd say something like: "You know, two years ago I used another company because I couldn't remember your company name and I lost your phone number." That's one of the worst things you can hear as a business owner—that someone used someone else, even though they loved your service, simply because they didn't remember you. That's what rebranding solves.

It makes you unforgettable—because when people connect to your personal story, and that story is tied to your business name, it's easy to remember.

Remember Plumbing Hounds? I didn't actually remember the business name at first. What I remembered was the cause. He volunteers at a dog shelter, and that stuck with me. I thought, *Okay, the guy works with dogs... Plumbing... Dogs? No—Plumbing Hounds!*

You see what I'm saying? I used to have a forgettable business. It wasn't until I tied my story into the business—and my business name into that story—that people started referring others to me by name. They'd say, "Use this company. Use him," instead of just saying, "Oh man, I know a guy... I wish I could remember his business name."

A rebrand or company story should include a strong community tie-in. It should tell a clear story, have a defined mission, and maintain a consistent association with a trusted local initiative.

Think about Firehouse Subs. It's a popular sandwich chain. But why "Firehouse"? Because when you walk in, there are pictures of firemen everywhere. Firemen are trusted figures in the U.S., so Firehouse Subs tied its brand to something people inherently trust. They even donate a portion of their funds to fire departments. That's why you remember the name.

So, find something you can tie to a trusted local initiative. And of course, be honest about it. If you're going to say it, you better do it. This is what leads to an irresistible identity.

It leads to:

- Memorability
- Increased referrals
- Brand clarity
- Long-term impact through brand consistency

Strong branding helps you scale faster by building recognition. And what does recognition do? It makes people remember you. "Oh, that's the business I always see at the local festival, handing out water!" That kind of recognition builds trust. And when people trust you, they buy from you, even if you're more expensive.

Customer Loyalty

Remember in the chapter where I talked about how the customer list is the gold mine? You can't build a solid customer list if people are constantly leaving your business. But a strong brand—one that's tied to the community, that's trusted, and that has a compelling story— keeps people coming back, even when there are cheaper alternatives.

Even when competitors knock on their door, people stay loyal to you because they're emotionally tied to your story. You don't want to be just a business that does [XYZ]. You want to be the business that feels like a person—a member of the community where your customers live and work every day.

Brand Consistency

Brand consistency means using the same tone, voice, and message across all platforms: your emails, your website, your printed materials.

What does that mean?

Okay, remember when I said you don't want to create your customer story, your brand colors, and your brand name, and then just write them in a notebook, close it, and forget about it? That's pointless.

Your customer or brand story is the template you should use every single time you communicate, whether you're writing an email, sending a text message, or creating a web page. Every piece of communication should reflect that story in some way. Every time you hand out a flyer, that story should be there.

You want your visual identity on your trucks, uniforms, and ads to align with your story. Everything should tie back to it.

I mentioned Firehouse Subs as an example. Everywhere you see them, there's some reference to firefighters. Why? Because they want to make their brand sticky, memorable, and irresistible.

That's the kind of consistency you should aim for in your storytelling and messaging. Use the brand story you've created—one that is unique to you. Why? Because that's how you frustrate your competitors. If you write a story that's authentic and unique to your business, it can't be copied.

And if they can't copy you, they can't compete with you. In conclusion: give your brand teeth. Tell a story only you can tell. This will make your brand visible. It'll make it memorable. It'll make it emotionally resonant. And when your brand resonates, customers won't shop around. They'll remember you, and they'll choose you.

Brand Character

Your company's voice should reflect its character. So, what do I mean by that? Let's say your brand identity is fun-loving, childlike, or innocent. Maybe your logo features a cartoon character, and you enjoy keeping things lighthearted. In that case, your emails should also be fun. They can be goofy, playful, and full of personality—if that's the story your brand is built on.

But let's say your brand has a more serious tone. Maybe your company is focused on a serious mission or cause. In that case, your messaging—emails, ads, social media—should also be serious and purposeful. Of course, we must be careful with overly serious messaging; we don't want to overwhelm or depress people. But once you define who your company is, your tone should reflect that consistently.

Take Gillette, for example. For a long time, their branding focused on inspiring men. Their ads featured lines like, "You can be the man who climbs the highest mountain." The music was uplifting, and the message was clear. It was serious and inspirational. Not every brand needs to take that approach, but Gillette stayed true to its character, and its voice aligned perfectly.

Now contrast that with Toys R Us. Remember that big ol' giraffe, Geoffrey? Their commercials were goofy and fun. The music was upbeat, kids were laughing and running around. It was all very child-friendly and playful. Why? Because their brand focused on children, and their voice reflected that consistently.

Your brand's voice should always reflect your company's character. Whether serious or silly, emotional or playful, consistency is what makes your message powerful and unforgettable.

Many companies in the home service business (heating, plumbing, electrical, landscaping, etc.) are smaller companies with fifty employees or fewer. A lot of times, we feel like the brand story is something meant for major corporations—McDonald's, Macy's—and we think, *We're a small company; that doesn't really work on a small scale.* But that's another mental block.

That's a limiting belief. Mainly, a lot of companies just don't believe that level of brand identity works on a small scale. But it definitely works—on any scale. As a matter of fact, it's probably even more effective on a small scale because none of the competitors are doing it.

A second challenge is a lack of belief that you can write a compelling story. Almost every time I talk to a client and say, "Hey, it's time to write your unique story," I'm confronted with a response like, "Well, I don't have an interesting story." And that's a limiting belief, because every person has a unique story that is interesting. You may not know how to tell it, but you have it.

So it's a mixture of not believing that it works on a small scale, or not believing that they have a story compelling enough to put out into the world. Once you know who your ideal customer is and how to attract them, the next step is figuring out *what to say*. Because if your message doesn't connect, they won't click, call, or care.

In the next chapter, we're diving into the power of messaging that sells—how to write and speak in a way that makes your company feel like the obvious choice.

CHAPTER 8

Messaging That Sells

What does "messaging that sells" really mean?

Messaging only works if there's clear value for the customer, also known as: "What's in it for me?" Whenever you're communicating with your customers, think of it like a relationship. No one enjoys a friendship, or any kind of relationship, where the other person only talks about themselves, focuses solely on their own benefits, or pushes only what works for them.

That's tiring. It's irritating. It's boring. You'd probably end that relationship as soon as you could. It's almost toxic. Well, when we're messaging our customers—when we're in a relationship with them— we want to make sure we're not that selfish person. We're not that bad boyfriend. The one who only cares about himself. We want to care about our customers, even to the point where our messaging is lopsided, focused almost entirely on them. Because let's face it, you're not married to your customers. This is, to a degree, a transactional relationship.

Of course, when I talk about branding, I emphasize making it relational. Your branding and messaging should create a sense of connection. But at the end of the day, it should still be focused on your customer and the things they care about. That's what I mean by "What's in it for me?"

Here's the truth: customers don't care about what you're offering. They're not excited that you started a business. They're not thrilled that you made a cool logo, slapped it on a shirt, and launched your first product. They're preoccupied with their own lives and their own needs.

And when they do need something, they go looking for a business that provides it. So message them with that in mind. They don't care about what you're selling—they care about what they're getting.

If they read your message and there's nothing in it for them—nothing they can use or benefit from—they won't engage. Worse, they might read it and then block you.

Here are some examples.

Weak offer: Guitars on sale!

Okay... who cares? I don't care if you're selling a guitar, unless I actually need one.

Strong offer: Play like you've always dreamed with our beginner-friendly guitar lessons.

Ooh. Isn't that better? You're not just selling something, you're promising an outcome your customer wants.

I think about my brother, who's in the music business. He has a large social media following, and his audience really grew when he shifted his messaging in this way. For example, he originally offered a class titled "Practice Like a Pro."

But seriously, who wants to practice? No one wakes up thinking, *I can't wait to practice.* There's no immediate value there. He changed the course title to "Play Like a Pro." That's a dream. That's what customers want. They don't want to practice today—they want to play like they've always dreamed. That's powerful messaging.

Here's an even stronger example: Boost your child's intellect with music lessons.

Now that resonates. Parents care more about their child's intellect than your guitar sale. The message focuses on what they care about, not what you're selling.

Here's one I used in my own business—in heating and cooling. We were always trying to get people to do maintenance on their systems. Maintenance is very important. But let's face it, nobody wakes up in the morning saying, "I really want to read about air conditioning." It's one of the most boring topics you can find.

But I have to generate revenue, so I have to make it interesting. That's why I don't just message people saying, "Hey, your air conditioner needs to be serviced." Who cares about that? Instead, my messaging looks more like:

Five Great Reasons to Service Your HVAC System.

1. Breathe cleaner air in your home.
2. Save money on electric bills.

Isn't that something your customer cares about?

Now, as the business owner, if my homeowners are breathing cleaner air, it doesn't affect me directly. But it affects them, and I'm writing to them. So I should write about things that matter to them. That's when you start to create really powerful messaging.

Business owners often struggle with this type of messaging because they write from their own point of view. We have a product, we're excited about it, we're passionate about it, and we know how important it is. But sometimes, that excitement doesn't translate to the customer. So often, businesses write from their own perspective, not the customer's.

That's the most common mistake.

As business owners, we often think we're the hero of the story. "Your electric bills are really high, and I'm the one who can solve it." But let's be honest, nobody wants to read about you being the hero. They want to be the hero. They want to win.

For example, many businesses, especially those in the trades, post pictures on social media of their trucks driving down the road. Why? Because they like how their trucks look. They've put a lot of effort into the design and are proud to have grown from one vehicle to six.

But your customer doesn't care that you went from one truck to six. And they don't care how fancy your truck looks. So stop posting images of your logos, and start posting things they care about. For example, a weak social media message might be a picture of your truck driving down the road.

A strong social media message? A video of your technician cooling down a hot house—and petting the family's puppy while they're at it. That's what people care about. That is powerful messaging.

It's not difficult. It's actually very fundamental.

Here's another mistake business owners often make: they wait for their marketing company to handle the messaging. They'll pay a billboard company to put up a sign in town, fork over $500, and the company slaps on a logo and calls it a day. Unfortunately, many marketers don't spend enough time crafting the message. Remember the section of this book where we talked about branding?

You know your company's story. You know your company's message. You know what you've consistently used to connect with your base. So, you need to take ownership when working with a marketing company. You should be the one saying, "When you put up my billboard, when you launch my Facebook ad, this is the message you're going to use." You have to take ownership. That's the only way to stay consistent.

Another mistake business owners often make is neglecting their day-to-day micro-messages. These include emails, phone calls, and outbound calls to your audience. Remember the section where I talked about your customer list? Those text messages we send, those outbound communications to our customer list, all those tiny, everyday messages are usually the ones that get overlooked. They're the ones who don't receive the care needed to ensure the right message is being delivered.

Sure, we remember the big stuff, like putting together a television commercial that highlights our reviews and showcases our volunteer work at the food shelter. That commercial runs once a year, and we might spend $100,000 on it. So, of course, we take time to craft it carefully. But what about the text messages you send throughout the year?

Even those small, micro-messages should follow a clear framework. Great messaging is essential, and it must be practiced across all customer touchpoints. Now, I'm not saying every text message you send should be four paragraphs long. That's not realistic. What I am saying is that we need to be mindful. Every message is an opportunity to tell your story and connect with the customer.

Getting Inside the Customer's Mind

Start by identifying your ideal customer. This is very important. Every person has their own background, culture, demographic traits, age, and even gender. Do they have a family? Are they single? These factors matter when crafting your message.

If you really dial into who your customer is, it becomes much easier to write a message that resonates. Here are some example questions you should ask when identifying your customer avatar:

- Do they have a family?
- What is their age group?
- What life stage are they in?

There's a huge difference between a nineteen-year-old college student and a sixty-year-old man with a wife and grandkids. They care about completely different things.

Even tone matters. There's a noticeable difference between how baby boomers respond to messaging and how millennials do. Baby boomers tend to prefer a more professional, formal tone. Millennials often favor a fun, relaxed, and informal voice—maybe even with some humor and irreverence. But if your customers are baby boomers, not millennials, you need to know that and adapt your tone accordingly. Also, ask yourself: *Are my customers price-conscious or luxury-focused?*

Do your customers have tons of money that they just throw around? If they do, and they only care about value and buying the best of the best, then maybe you shouldn't be messaging about discounts and budget-friendly options. They might scoff at that, close your message, and move on—or vice versa. If your customers are very price-conscious and don't prioritize premium value, then your messaging should focus more on affordability and pricing.

To take it a step further, if your customers are price-conscious, you might write messaging that educates them on the greater value of your higher-end offerings. You can help them shift their mindset by showing them the long-term benefits of choosing quality over cost.

What Annoys or Excites Your Customers?

Here's an exercise I want you to try when you're building your customer avatar. Get out a piece of paper. Personally, I like using notebooks because I'm old-school—I like to write things down and see them on paper. But if you'd rather do this on your phone or laptop, that's fine too. Just make sure you do it.

Start by writing down everything you can about your ideal customer. And be realistic. Everyone's ideal customer is a billionaire who throws money around, but let's bring it back to reality.

Who actually lives in your community? Who is truly going to buy from you? One thing you can do is go into your customer history and look at your revenue data. See which tickets were the highest, and which products or services brought in the most income. Then, look at those customers inside your CRM and gather as much information as you can about them.

For example, in my company, I looked at the top ten customers who spent the most over the last five years. I wrote down their names, their ages, whether they had families, whether they had spouses, kids, or grandkids, and even where they hung out. What I discovered was that nine out of ten of them were the same age, had similar family structures, and lived on the same side of town.

So guess what? I decided to start writing my messaging for that specific demographic. I want you to do the same. Take your top ten customers, write down their names, and list everything you know about them. Then look for patterns. Do certain traits or trends show up?

If they do, here's your next step: Name that avatar. Let's say nine out of ten of your top customers are over fifty, married, with kids in sports, and even grandkids. Then pick a name—make one up. Call them

"Bill." Or "Sally." Write that name down and keep it somewhere visible in your office.

Now, every time you go to write a message, whether it's a text, an email, a TV ad, or a Facebook ad, you're going to write it for "Bill," that fake customer who represents your real audience. You'll know how old "Bill" is, what he likes, and what kind of person he is because he's modeled after your best customers. When you write a message for that person, it will land better with your audience. You don't have to stick to just one customer avatar.

You can have five or six. You might have one older customer who values premium, high-ticket items. You might also have an avatar that is more budget-minded, so when you run discounts, you can tailor your message to that customer.

Just make sure you name each one so you don't forget. I love this technique because it's visual and helps me stay focused. When I see those names, I immediately know who I'm writing for.

Here's a real-life example. A young man came to my door recently. He was trying to sell me pest control. This young man was from a completely different demographic from me, and he had a hard time connecting. But he kept trying. He continued asking me questions, over and over.

"Do you have moles?"

"No, I don't have moles."

"Do you have fire ants?"

I told him I hadn't seen a fire ant on my property in twenty years. He kept asking and asking, until finally, he asked about mosquitoes.

And I hate mosquitoes. I wish they'd be wiped off the planet. *Boom!* That was his instant connection.

Now, do you think he talked about moles again after he saw my soul light up at the mention of mosquitoes? Nope. He never mentioned moles again. Never brought up ants either.

From that moment on, everything he said was about mosquitoes. And just like that, he went from being unable to connect with me to capturing my full attention, as if he were starring in a Hollywood film. Why? Because he discovered what resonated with me. Is this what's happening when you're writing emails and messages?

Are people connecting? Do you know what they actually like or dislike? Do you want your messages to fall flat, or do you want your audience riveted, hanging on your every word, because they feel like you're speaking directly to them?

This young man connected with me because he dug in to find out what mattered to me, the customer. That's the entire point I want to get across to you: Always highlight the desire behind the purchase, not just the product.

This young door-to-door pest control salesman could have just said, "Hey, I can get rid of pests. It'll be $500." But he didn't. He dug deeper. He found what I cared about—getting rid of mosquitoes. He didn't even talk about pest control anymore. He started talking about how he hates mosquitoes and how he could get rid of them.

So, don't just talk about your product. Find the desires of your customer, and write messages that speak to those desires.

Another example: I was recently at a business meeting with a group of business owners. We were discussing messaging, specifically postcards. I send hundreds of postcards every month to my community, and I asked: "What do you guys do to keep people from tossing your postcards straight into the circular file?" (You know, the trash can.)

Something one of the guys said really stuck with me. He owns a pressure washing company. He said the postcard that brings in the most business for him had this headline: *"Don't be the dirtiest house on the block."* That postcard outperformed his others tenfold. Way more than the typical: *"Pressure washing discount! $59 if you use this!"* Because nobody cares about your pressure washing or your discount. What they do care about is not being the dirtiest house on the block. He tapped into something emotional—an insecurity, a social trigger. People don't want to be the neighborhood gossip topic because of a dirty house.

Structure for clear, compelling messaging. Here's a messaging formula I use:

The Four Pillars of a Good Message

A strong message is built on four key pillars:

1. Identify Yourself

Who are you? Who's texting or emailing the customer?

For example: "Hey, this is Michael from Acme Plumbing."

Simple, clear, and establishes trust right away.

2. Communicate the Benefit

Why should the customer keep reading? What's in it for them?

For instance: "Did you know that unattended leaky pipes can grow mold, which can be harmful to your family?"

Now you've got their attention. You've made it relevant to their life.

3. Add Urgency or Limited Availability

Give them a reason to act now.

For example: "This week only, we're offering free pipe inspections to check for mold."

Now the customer knows there's a deadline. They need to respond this week—or miss out. Without urgency, they might read your message, feel concerned, and then just forget about it.

4. End with a Clear Call to Action

Close your message with an open-ended question that invites a response.

Example: "Would you like me to schedule your plumbing inspection today?"

Boom! You've now got a compelling, complete message that invites engagement.

When your message includes all four pillars, you will get attention, and more importantly, action. You'll get people calling you. Make it a habit to include all four elements every time you send a message. Once you do, you can start testing and optimizing. Send messages out, track the responses, and tweak one element at a time to increase your closing rate.

Consistency is key. Remember what I said about the sales process? If you follow a consistent process, it becomes easy to adjust small details and measure what works. But if you're just sending random messages, you won't know what's making an impact, and you won't be able to improve. So keep your messages consistent. Use the Four Pillars, then experiment by adjusting them slightly. Over time, you'll discover what makes your message powerful.

I write messages like this for my coaching clients. One example: I worked with an HVAC company that had been texting their customers for years, with almost zero response. Once we restructured their messages using these four pillars, everything changed.

I reviewed their message and said, "Hey, you don't have anything in here except information about you." So we restructured it using the Four Pillars. And guess what? Just by changing the messaging, they sold thousands of dollars in just a few days.

Now apply this approach to your email campaigns. Apply it to your website copy. Apply it to your social media posts.

This is psychology that works. Messaging and sales go hand in hand. Remember: when messaging fails, sales stall, because there's no emotional connection or practical hook.

All four of those pillars are very important. Take the open-ended question at the end—most people, if they get a text message from an actual person, will respond. That's why I said you have to include Pillar Number One: Who are you? Because if you say, *"This is Mike's Auto Shop,"* well, that's a business. No one has to respond to a business. But if you say, *"Hey, this is Sarah from Mike's Auto Shop,"* followed by: *"Would you like me to schedule you today?"* most people will want to respond. Why? Because it feels rude not to. And they're either going to say, *"Yes, schedule me today,"* or *"No."*

If they say yes, you schedule them. If they say no, you follow up with: *"Okay, when would be a good day for you?"* That's how good messaging works.

Now, you can test your messaging through A/B testing. If your message is consistent, you can change just one word here and there, and then track the results.

When it comes to results, whether it's branding, sales, or messaging, you're going to be testing and tweaking constantly. And that cycle—tweaking, testing, reviewing results—is something you'll do for the rest of your business life, until you arrive at something truly powerful.

That's going to be your secret sauce—the unique edge in your business that no one else has.

Common Messaging Mistakes

Messages are often:

- Too vague

- Too generic
- Full of company-centered language

You know, like that self-centered person in a relationship who only wants to talk about themselves. That's how a lot of business messaging comes across. Most poor messaging is missing one or more of the Four Pillars of a good message.

Rework your messages to focus on the customer. Use emotion. Use the things they care about, not what you care about. You want emotional resonance and clarity.

Emotion is what moves people to act. I recently completed a big job, and it's one of my favorite stories from my business. It was a really, really big project. And after every job we do, we ask two questions:

1. How did you hear about us?—that's a marketing question.
2. Why did you choose us?—and that's the one most businesses don't ask.

Most companies track how their customers found them, but they don't track why the customer actually chose them. So after we completed this job, I asked the client, "We gave you the quote, and you decided to go with us. Why did you choose us over the other three bids?"

And the guy said, "Because you sent me a Christmas message."

Isn't that amazing? He chose us over two other companies, just because I sent him a Christmas message. People buy because of emotional and human connections. Never forget that. It's true today, and it will still be true 100 years from now.

Here's an example of a social media post I've used for years. I post it every single year, at the same time, and it always works. It says: *"Hi, my name is Michael. I was born on a shelf in a hardware store."* It goes on to say that I worked with my father, who is a longtime tradesman. He's seventy-six years old and still working. I worked with my father from the time I was a kid until I joined the United States Air Force, where I learned the heating and air conditioning trade. It's been twenty years since I started, and now we have over 800 five-star reviews. I even posted a picture of myself and my father.

I put that on Facebook and all the local groups, and it always brings in business. Why? Because it creates a human connection.

Sure, I could post a picture of an air conditioner and say, *"Do you need air conditioning? We're here."* That's what I see every day. But that's boring. Do you see how many social cues my own message includes? I was born on a shelf in a hardware store—that's credibility. I'm the son of a tradesman—more credibility. Learned heating and cooling in the United States Air Force, even more. Twenty years in the business, over 800 five-star reviews, it's a cascade of credibility statements. After reading that short paragraph, you've seen seven or eight reasons to trust me.

But what does the customer really care about? Do they care about the details of my resume? No. They care about who's coming into their home and working on their most expensive appliance.

Why does this work? Because it builds instant trust. It evokes nostalgia. It taps into patriotism. And it tells a story without sounding like a sales pitch. This is messaging that converts. You want to inform and explain, because when people understand more, they feel more comfortable. And when people are more comfortable, they are more likely to buy.

Use your messaging to inspire people.

Use it to create curiosity or to reinforce trust and identity, both before and after an SMS campaign. Remember the client I had in my coaching program who had been texting for years with no results? We changed just one element—we added an open-ended question, and it made all the difference.

Sometimes, the money you're spending on ads isn't being wasted because the platform doesn't work. It's because your messaging was bad. One change can shift everything forever.

Say what your customer is already thinking. Make your messaging customer-centered, make it emotional, make it testable. Use your personal story—the one you developed during the branding exercise—to anchor credibility and trust.

When you speak your customer's language, they will listen. And they will buy. That's it.

The first pillar is always telling people who you are—and it has to come first in the message, no exceptions.

Here's why: people are bombarded by messaging. The first thing they think is, *Is this a stranger talking to me?* So, you need to state who you are right away.

I like to remind people of the relationship we already have. For example: "Hey, this is Michael from Acme Plumbing. We worked on your HVAC system two months ago." *Boom!* I'm no longer a stranger. They remember me: *Hey, this person did work on my system.*

When people know you, they're more likely to listen to you. Imagine you're walking down the street and someone stops you and says, "Hey, how are you doing? Can I ask you a question?" You probably don't want to talk to them. But what if they said, "Hey, I think we went to elementary school together—first grade. Can I ask you a question?" Okay, now you're listening. When people know who you are, and know that you're a real person, not just some autobot messaging them, they're much more likely to read the rest of your message.

Now, the fourth pillar—an open-ended question—must be the last thing in the message. It has to be. If you put your open-ended question in the middle, they'll read it, then continue reading the rest of the message and forget that you even asked a question. You want to leave them hanging—you want to put the ball in their court.

If you don't ask an open-ended question, they'll read your message and think, *Wow, that was a good text message,* and then go on with their day. But if you do ask one, they'll feel compelled to respond. You're giving them the responsibility to end the conversation by replying. So it's super important.

Pillar number one has to be number one.

Pillar number four has to be number four.

Pillars two and three can switch places, if necessary.

CHAPTER 9

Ground Game Marketing and Tracking

Introduction to Ground Game Marketing

This idea is inspired by my military experience. I served six years in the military and was on active duty when the United States invaded Iraq and Afghanistan.

I was twenty-four years old, and I'll never forget the moment we shifted from a peacetime military to a wartime posture. I witnessed firsthand what makes a tactic effective.

The first thing our military does is build a strong ground game. We invade, establish a presence, and get boots on the ground. You can't take control of a territory without that foundational presence.

Now, to be clear, I'm not a warmonger. I don't believe in war. I wish we lived in a world without it. But warfare teaches tactical principles that we can learn from. Because think about it—you're trying to take ground in your community.

I'm always deeply impressed when I meet soldiers who've taken ground with a small team, sometimes just seven or eight people. I'll never forget the time I pulled a soldier aside and said: "I'm trying to take territory for my business. I'm trying to gain market share, and I'm struggling. But I know that during the war, when we were in the military together, you went into a city with a team of five or six people and took it. How in the world can you do that with six people, and here I am, with nobody shooting at me or trying to blow me up, and I still can't capture market share?"

What I learned from that conversation was fundamental: it's all about ground tactics.

Ground tactics in business are the things we don't like to do. So, get ready—you're probably about to read some things you're not going to want to do. But those very things are the ones that will make the biggest difference in your business.

Why? Because the things you don't want to do are probably the same things your competition doesn't want to do either. If your competition doesn't want to do it, there's a pretty good chance they're not doing it, meaning there's an opportunity for you to be the only one who is.

Ground-level strategies are actions you can execute immediately without relying on any outside agency. Take Facebook, for example. When I post in a local group, I have to rely on Facebook to even show that post to people. The algorithm has all the power. If I create a YouTube video about my business, it might never show up in someone's feed. YouTube controls that visibility.

Or, say I hire a marketing company to do search engine optimization (SEO) so that my website appears when people search for my product. I still have to hope that the marketing company does a good job. And even if they do, I have to hope Google rewards it and actually shows my site. The truth is, many of the methods we use to get business are completely out of our control.

But not everything is. There are still actions that are in your control—things only you can do. These are what I call "ground tactics."

Examples of Ground Tactics:

Door Knocking

Where are the people you're trying to reach? There's one place they go every single day: home. They might not log into Facebook today. They might skip Instagram or TikTok. But they'll go home. And all you have to do is knock on their door.

Is it scary? Yes. Is it effective? You bet it is.

But remember, if you're going to knock on doors, your messaging better be dialed in. If you make it about yourself, you'll likely have a poor experience. But if you make it about them, it changes everything.

Think about that pest control guy who came to my door. He talked about things I cared about, like getting rid of mosquitoes. I didn't mind him knocking. But if he had just pitched his company with no relevance to me, I wouldn't have been interested.

Calling and Texting Past Customers

This is another ground tactic. Nothing is stopping you from picking up the phone and calling your customers. You already have their numbers—you don't need to pay a marketing company to find them.

They're sitting right in your CRM. Open your laptop, start from the top, and begin calling.

When you do, use the Four Pillars:

"Hey, this is Michael from Acme Plumbing. I was at your house three months ago. I just wanted to let you know we're running a special, but it's only available through Friday. We're doing free inspections. Can I schedule you?"

Boom! Simple, quick, easy.

No algorithm to worry about. You're in complete control.

Networking in Your Community

Go where your customers go. Attend festivals, local events, and networking meetings.

Let's say you own a heating and cooling company. You're driving to Chipotle for a burrito, and you see a guy mowing lawns. Stop. Ask for his business card, and give him yours. That interaction was easy and free.

This is the ground game. These are ground tactics. They put the power back in your hands and don't require you to wait, pay, or hope someone else does the job right.

Every time you see a business owner, you should ask them for their business card, and you should give them yours, because they're fellow business owners. They understand you, and they understand the need for referrals. No one's going to turn you down if you ask for their business card. And guess what? We're using psychology. If I ask you for your business card because I want to refer you to my friend, and then I turn around and say, "Hey, would you refer me?" you pretty much have to say yes. At the very least, they'll take your card. And now that's another person who knows about your business. Consistent follow-ups and staying top of mind—this is a ground tactic.

Part of the sales process is follow-ups. Do you see how all of this ties together? Nothing is stopping you from following up with your customers.

Nothing is stopping you from messaging your customers consistently. That's the ground game. I don't have to worry about Facebook not putting my post in front of people.

You know the frustration. You post something, and nobody sees it, even though you have a thousand followers. Let's take the power away from these big organizations and put it in your own hands as a business owner.

Now, I know what you're thinking: *Well, I'm an introvert, and you know I'm not good at door-knocking.* Who cares? You need revenue, and you need it fast, and this works.

And you know what? I'll let you in on a little secret: The more you do it, the better you'll get at it.

Here are some common mistakes when it comes to ground tactics:

Relying Too Heavily on Digital Paid Media

Why do we rely so heavily on buying ads—Facebook ads, television ads? Because it's easy. Because it allows us to make excuses for ourselves. I can't tell you how many of my business consulting clients have told me:

- "Well, Michael, I can't go to networking meetings because I'm shy."
- "I can't door-knock because it's going to irritate people."
- "I'm an introvert."

And so on.

So they just take their money, give it to some rich corporation, and run ads. Then they show up at business meetings and say, "My ads aren't working." The ground game works. You cannot take territory without getting on the ground.

Not Building a Local Presence or Community Brand Awareness

Your customers are literally at the local concert. They're literally at the local fair. In our town, we have a local food festival. There are tens of thousands of people there. I would love for tens of thousands of people to know about my business. So I'm going to go. I'm going to go there as a business, set up a table, give away water, hand out cards, and hold a little contest in exchange for their name, email, and phone number.

Only Reaching Out When Revenue Is Low

I call this the "12th-round mindset." The 12th-round mindset means this: imagine you're in a boxing match. You've gone through the first 11 rounds, and you didn't even try to punch back—you just took hits the whole time. Now it's the 12th round, the fight is almost over, and suddenly you think, *Man, I've got to fight to win.*

Well, it's kind of late. You're already beat up.

Don't wait until you're desperate to take action. Don't rely on marketing or ground tactics only when you need money. You should be doing this even when business is booming, even when your bank account is full. Because if you wait until it's too late, you'll already be too beaten down to make a real change, and the opportunity may have passed.

Avoid a 12-round or 11-hour mentality. Focus on results. Everything we do—whether spending money or time—is about creating opportunities. If you're messaging customers, that's an opportunity. You don't want to waste it. Don't go out door-knocking, attending networking events, or messaging your customer base without tracking what's working. Wouldn't you want your efforts to get better and better over time? That's where results come in.

I call it the "Test, Tweak, Test, Tweak" method. Let's say you knock on ten doors using the Four Pillars. If all ten people curse you out, you're in the test phase. Now you tweak—maybe you take a step back from the door to give people space. Try again.

Now, only eight out of ten curse you out. You've improved. Eventually, you'll be closing deals—but you won't know what's working unless you track the results. In every ground tactic you use, track the results. Be consistent. Test, evaluate, tweak, and repeat.

Think like a coach. Every good coach knows the score during the game. One of my sons plays basketball, another boxes, and another plays soccer. And in sports like basketball and soccer—where points matter—any coach can tell you the score at any moment.

Imagine a coach waiting until the game ends and then asking, "Did we win?" That would be a terrible coach. Why? Because by then, it's too late to make adjustments.

Your KPIs (Key Performance Indicators) are the scoreboard for your business. If you're cold calling and ten out of ten hang up, you have a 0% conversion rate. Tweak one thing, and now one out of ten stays on the line—you're at 10%. That's progress.

Track your score. Otherwise, you're not coaching your business—you're guessing.

What should you be tracking?

New Customers Per Month

If you're getting zero, it's time to examine your marketing. If you're getting a lot, double down on what's working.

Average Ticket Size

This is crucial. Is the average sale amount going up or down? If it was $1,000 in March and dropped to $200 in April, something's wrong—and if you don't catch it in time, you could be in trouble.

Average Sale Per Employee

Another big one. This can show where individual or team performance is thriving, or where it's lagging.

If we only look at our average sales across all employees, the high performers might be hiding the underperformers. That's why you need to track average sales per employee. If one employee averages

$1,000 per sale and another averages $1 per sale, you should take a closer look.

You might want to have the underperforming employee shadow the high performer, or vice versa, to learn and improve.

Booking Rates

For every person who calls your business, what percentage actually gets scheduled on the calendar? For every person who walks into your store, what percentage makes a purchase?

Email Open Rates

Are people even opening your emails? Do they open them more often when you use the Four Pillars compared to when you don't? You need to test that so you can see the difference.

Text Message Response Rates

This is why I don't believe in sending a mass text message to your entire customer base. If you have 10,000 customers, don't blast the same message to all 10,000. Instead, send one message to 100 people and measure the response rate. Then tweak the message. Send it to another 100. Keep repeating this process until you reach your desired response rate.

Only then should you send that final, optimized message to all 10,000, or whatever portion remains.

Profit Margins

You also need to monitor your profit margins—a critical part of knowing your numbers. I go deeper into this in my private business coaching community, because it's that important.

In fact, it's so important that I wouldn't even attempt to cover it all in a single chapter. This is something you should work on regularly with a mentor or coach. The "test, tweak, track" method only works if you check your results.

Tracking is a lot like reading the Bible, whether you read it or not, hear me out. Sometimes when people read the Bible and see what Jesus taught, they feel convicted because they realize they're not living up to it. But feeling that discomfort can be a good thing. It shows you where you need to grow.

The same goes for tracking your results. You might be scared to look at them because you already know they're bad. But facing them is the only way to feel that momentary sting—and then get fired up to make a change.

We're living in the greatest time in the world. We have tools to help us do all of the things I'm talking about—tracking this, tracking that, writing messages, applying the Four Pillars, crafting emails, sending newsletters, and making sure your text messages are going out.

It's a lot. As a business owner, you're either going to get swamped or you'll need to hire someone just to handle all of it.

Or, you can hire someone and make their job easier by embracing technology. We're not trying to overwhelm our employees; we're saying, "Hey, here's what I want you to be responsible for, and here are some tools to make that easier."

You're still going to need to put boots on the ground, but when it comes to tracking results, I recommend investing in the right software:

- *Mass Text Messaging:* I had a client with 2,000 customers who wrote every message individually on their iPhone, changing each name manually. Can you imagine doing that 2,000 times? There's software that can send personalized messages to all 2,000 people in one go.

- *Message Scheduling:* You can write text messages now and schedule them five or six years in advance. Isn't that amazing?

- *Ringless Voicemail:* Record one message and have it dropped straight into someone's voicemail box. They wake up, check their phone, and there's your message—with your voice, creating a real human connection.

- *Email Marketing Tools:* These platforms make staying in touch simple and effective.

Long story short: Embrace technology.

How to choose the right tech? It's actually very easy. Write down everything you do repeatedly. Then ask yourself: *Is there software that can do this for me automatically if I set it up once?* If the answer is yes— use it. It will free you from being the overworked, constantly stressed business owner.

Why does ground game marketing work? Because it saves money by reducing your dependency on expensive, uncontrollable marketing. The power is now in your hands.

It also builds traction through story-led differentiation and real human interaction. Remember that—human interaction—before the pandemic, when we all became so disconnected? One of the things people crave most is exactly that. You can create meaningful human interaction within your business by connecting with your customers through a ground game: boots on the ground, networking, and engaging in as many conversations as possible.

The Consequences of Skipping Ground Game Marketing

When you skip foundational steps you risk having incomplete growth strategies. You might end up pouring money into digital marketing without a solid base, leading to a high customer acquisition cost (CAC).

CAC is the amount you spend to acquire a customer. For example, if you spend $1,000 on Facebook ads and gain ten customers, your CAC is $100. But what if you spent that same $1,000 attending a festival and collected 10,000 names and email addresses? Your CAC would drop significantly, giving you a much stronger return on investment.

Skipping the ground game marketing steps leads to more than just high costs. It weakens your brand presence. When someone scrolls past your ad on Facebook or Instagram, if the algorithm even shows it to them, it's not the same as having a personal interaction. Ground game marketing isn't just a framework—it's a mindset. When applied consistently, it helps build a business that grows fast, scales smart, and stands out in any market.

CHAPTER 10

The Profit Playbook

Back when I was just starting out, there were days I'd sit in my truck at the end of the day and think, *We had a full schedule, everyone worked hard… so why is there no money in the account?* Sound familiar?

I wasn't lazy. My techs weren't slacking. Customers were happy. But the bank account didn't lie—something wasn't adding up.

At first, I chalked it up to the usual excuses: "It's just a slow season." "Customers are being cheap." "My team needs to try harder." But deep down, I knew the truth: I didn't have a way to *measure* what was working and what wasn't. And because I couldn't measure it, I couldn't fix it.

It wasn't until I started building what I now call my **Profit Playbook** that I truly began to understand the business side of HVAC. I stopped running my company off gut feelings and started using math. Real numbers. KPIs. Expectations. Just like I would if I were troubleshooting a compressor issue or diagnosing a low airflow problem, I started tracking what the system was *supposed* to be doing.

And once I knew what the business *should* be doing, I could finally figure out why it wasn't.

A Business Should Run Like a Well-Tuned System

In HVAC, you already know how to diagnose systems. If a unit's not cooling, you check static pressure, subcooling, airflow—you don't just add refrigerant and hope for the best.

Your business is no different. It's a system. And like any system, it runs on predictable inputs and outputs. When one part underperforms, the whole thing suffers. The challenge is that most business owners don't know what the expected "readings" should be for each part of their company.

That's where the Profit Playbook comes in.

It All Starts with Pricing

Your entire business hinges on what you charge.

Let's say your overhead and margin structure require you to generate $300 in revenue per billable hour. That becomes your baseline. That's your "operating pressure," if we're sticking with the HVAC analogy. If your team isn't hitting that per hour, something's off.

Now, if your average service call takes 1.5 hours, that call needs to bring in $450 to keep the system running properly. That's your expected outcome.

If each tech runs four service calls a day, that's $1,800 per tech, per day in revenue. If you've got three trucks running, that's $5,400 in expected daily revenue.

So now, instead of hoping you make money this week, you know what *should* happen. And that gives you the power to fix it when it doesn't.

Now Tie It to the Office

Your techs aren't the only ones who need a target. The office plays just as critical a role in hitting those numbers.

If each tech needs four booked calls per day to hit their revenue target, then someone in the office needs to make sure those calls are actually on the board. That's their KPI. Their version of "static pressure."

Without those four booked jobs per tech, you're running a low-capacity system. You're under-loaded. And that's not a tech problem—it's an admin or call center problem.

Suddenly, you're not just pointing fingers. You're pinpointing *real issues* based on measurable expectations.

Then Bring in the CSRs

Now let's move upstream—right to your front line: your CSRs.

If they're only booking one out of every three calls that come in, that's a 33% booking rate. That means to book four jobs per day for one tech, you need twelve inbound leads that day. If you've got three techs on the schedule, you need thirty-six leads to fill the day. Not "hope for the phone to ring" leads. Actual, qualified, bookable leads.

So, if your CSRs are falling short on bookings, it's not because you don't have enough leads—it's because something's breaking in the call conversion process. Maybe they aren't answering fast enough. Maybe they're saying the wrong things. Maybe they're giving too many options or not asking for the appointment.

The point is: you now have visibility. You can *see* where the system is leaking.

And just like in HVAC, when you know what your readings should be, you stop guessing.

Marketing is Measurable, Too

Let's keep going. What happens if your CSRs are trained and doing great, but they're only getting six leads a day instead of twelve?

Then you don't have a conversion problem—you have a **lead generation** problem. That's a marketing issue. Whether it's your Google ads, your website, your direct mail, or your reputation management, something isn't generating enough attention to keep the system fueled.

But again, you don't have to guess. Because you've got a Profit Playbook.

The Full Funnel, Diagnosed Like a Pro

Let me simplify it:

- If you have enough leads but no bookings, you have a CSR problem.

- If you have bookings but not enough revenue, it's either a pricing or sales problem.
- If you don't have enough leads, you've got a marketing problem.
- If the techs are booked but can't finish jobs, you have a training or efficiency problem.

You are now officially in control because the Profit Playbook takes the emotion out of decision-making and replaces it with math.

You're no longer reacting—you're adjusting.

You're no longer confused—you're confident.

This is What Ownership Looks Like

When you know what your business is *supposed* to do at each stage, you can finally operate like an owner, not a firefighter. You stop throwing money at problems and start investing in precision. You stop panicking over a slow week and start solving the right problem.

But you can't get there without clarity.

You can't lead a business if you don't know what success looks like at each position.

So, here's what I recommend you do this week:

1. **Set your hourly revenue target per truck.**
   Know what number keeps you profitable.

2. **Estimate how many calls per day your techs can realistically run.**

    Don't be optimistic. Be honest.

3. **Do the math and get a daily revenue target.**

    Multiply the hourly rate × average hours per call × calls per day.

4. **Look at your CSR booking rate.**

    Track how many calls come in and how many actually get booked.

5. **Back-calculate how many leads per day you need.**

    If your CSRs close at 30%, and you need eight jobs booked per day, you'll need twenty-seven leads.

6. **Assign every department their KPI.**

    Techs = revenue per day.

    Office = jobs booked per day.

    CSRs = conversion percentage.

    Marketing = qualified leads per day.

Now you've got a system.

And when you have a system, you can finally get predictable results.

You can grow without chaos.

You can diagnose instead of guessing.

You can stop saying, "I feel like things are off," and start saying, "Here's where we're leaking, and here's what we're going to do about it."

If there's one truth I've learned from years of running my business and helping others fix theirs, it's this:

What you don't measure will eventually hurt you.

But when you know your numbers, you get your power back.

You stop being at the mercy of the market, the weather, or the season, and you start being the owner you were always meant to be.

That's the power of your Profit Playbook.

Conclusion

We've just covered the most powerful strategies I know — the ones that can transform your business the fastest. They've worked wonders for mine, and I've seen them create incredible results for the businesses I consult, time and time again. These are true needle-movers. I know they work. They've worked for me, and they can absolutely work for you.

So, I want to sincerely thank you and congratulate you for taking the time to read this and for investing in yourself. That commitment matters. I believe in you. I know you're going to take action, change your business, and ultimately, change the world.

There's a world of possibility ahead if you take these strategies and implement them. I've seen people 10x their business by applying just one of these principles.

If you're excited, inspired, and ready to make meaningful changes, I have an invitation for you: You can talk with me personally. I actively consult with businesses and am open to a one-on-one meeting. Simply scan the QR code:

From there, you can schedule a time with me. We'll chat, and I'll share how my coaching program can help you go even deeper with the ideas in this book—and get even greater results.

I'm looking forward to connecting with you.

Thank you again.

THANK YOU FOR READING MY BOOK!

DOWNLOAD YOUR FREE GIFTS

Just to say thanks for buying and reading my book, I would like to give you a few free bonus gifts, no strings attached!

Scan the QR Code:

I appreciate your interest in my book and value your feedback, as it helps me improve future versions. I would appreciate it if you could leave your invaluable review on Amazon.com with your feedback. Thank you!

www.ingramcontent.com/pod-product-compliance
Lightning Source LLC
Chambersburg PA
CBHW020205200326
41521CB00005BA/254